New Insights with Instant Handwriting Analysis

Of the many disciplines available to those who seek self-awareness and improvement, graphology is one of the most accurate and enjoyable. Although it will take more than a quick read-through for you to be able to discern all of your personality characteristics, an hour or two will give you many insights. You will certainly see many positive traits that you previously ignored. You may also see a number of characteristics that obstruct success in your passage through life.

Instant Handwriting Analysis lists many resources for continuing study in graphology, and several correspondence schools. You will also find additional resources for further study in associated fields. Some of those associated fields mentioned are document examination, intelligence determination and personnel selection.

The included overlayment transparencies will simplify accurate measurement of letters, parts of letters, degree of slant, spaces, margins and other variations in writing samples for precise analysis.

A dictionary chapter of meaningful letter formations can give you some instant feedback as to the meaning of some of your unique letter styles. You will be able to look up that unusual configuration that you always wondered about. You may want to change it to something that influences you in a more positive way, or you may be happy with it just the way it is. If you are dissatisfied with your signature, you can design a new one that feels more satisfactory, and in addition, better understand some of the meanings of both the old and the new.

Graphology is an exciting and useful key to aid in unlocking the potential within you. I wish you delight, success and satisfaction in your endeavor.

—*Ruth Gardner*

About the Author

Ruth Gardner was born on a South Dakota prairie farm in 1933. She was educated in a one-room schoolhouse through the eighth grade, and as a young girl she fed and milked cows, herded cattle, stacked hay and drove horse teams. Later she migrated to St. Paul to study nursing, and became an R.N. at age 20. In 1969 she began studying, and eventually teaching, graphology.

Ms. Gardner has a B.A. in Human Services, has been a consultant in areas of personal development, and is nationally accredited in biofeedback. She also has worked in a therapeutic massage clinic, instructing staff and clients in stress management.

In 1985 Ruth and her husband sold their home and purchased a 52-foot houseboat which they named Ra, after the Egyptian sun god. The Gardners moved aboard the houseboat and several months later cruised down the Mississippi, the Ohio, the Tennessee, the Tombigbee, and the Mobile rivers and out into the Gulf of Mexico. Eventually they went inland on the Caloosahatchee River to Ft. Meyers, LaBelle, and Moore Haven (on Lake Okeechobee), Florida, living in each place a few months.

After finishing her trip, Ms. Gardner returned to St. Paul and wrote *Instant Handwriting Analysis*.

To Write to the Author

If you wish to contact the author or would like more information about this book, please write to the author in care of Llewellyn Worldwide, and we will forward your request. The author and publisher appreciate hearing from you and learning of your enjoyment of this book and how it has helped you. Llewellyn Worldwide cannot guarantee that every letter written to the authors can answered, but all will be forwarded. Please write to:

Ruth Gardner
c/o Llewellyn Worldwide
P.O. Box 64383, Dept. L251-9, St. Paul, MN 55164-0383, U.S.A.

Please enclose a self-addressed, stamped envelope for reply, or $1.00 to cover costs.
If outside the U.S.A., enclose international postal reply coupon.

LLEWELLYN'S SELF-HELP SERIES

Instant Handwriting Analysis

A Key to Personal Success

by

Ruth Gardner

1997
Llewellyn Publications
St. Paul, Minnesota, 55164-0383, U.S.A.

Cover Art by Christopher Wells

FIRST EDITION
Fifth Printing, 1997

Library of Congress Cataloging-in-Publication Data
Gardner, Ruth, 1933–
   Instant handwriting analysis.
   (Llewellyn's self-help series)
   Bibliography: p.
   1. Graphology. 2. Success—Psychological aspects.
1. Title. II. Series.
BF891.G38   1989   155.2'82   89-12482
ISBN 0-87542-251-9

Llewellyn Publications
A Division of Llewellyn Worldwide, Ltd.
P.O. Box 64383, St. Paul, MN 55164-0383

LLEWELLYN'S SELF-HELP SERIES

We all search for ways to succeed in our lives. The success we search for in business, relationships, self-image, and other areas often depends on information. One of the most often used methods of finding information which will guide us to greater success is through feedback. We often request feedback from friends, relatives, and co-workers and then attempt to sort out what is factual and what might be highly colored by the feedback-giver.

Employers often call their feedback "constructive criticism." Sometimes it is constructive and sometimes it is not. However, whether the feedback is constructive or not, one of the most valuable tools we have for greater success is information leading to self-awareness. With such information we can begin to change some of the aspects of our personality that have impeded our progress.

One of the books in Llewellyn's Self-Help Series is *Instant Handwriting Analysis*, which deals with graphology. Graphology is a made-to-order key to opening our inner selves and exploring options for behavior change. With practice, one can make graphology an objective method of giving feedback to oneself. *It is important to be aware that it is possible for explorers of personal behavior to close their eyes to obvious deficiencies or defeating behaviors in themselves unless a truly open mind is kept.* Using the insights of graphology explained in this book can provide the reader with the means to acquire that most important of analytical tools—unbiased feedback.

Once the reader has discovered and accepted that important information, she/he can take steps to change behavior with the goal of personal success. Graphology offers an unbeatable channel to continue monitoring personal progress toward success.

Other books by the author:

A Graphology Student's Workbook

Edited and coordinated publication of

The Women's Network Directory

Dedicated To

Ron,

My Students,

and

My Clients,

who have always

been my teachers

Contents

Author's Note Regarding Gender

In this work when the text generally refers to either masculine or feminine gender, the reader will find the pronouns "she" and "her" used exclusively. Both of those pronouns contain within them the pronoun "he." Although the objective "him" and the possessive "his" will not be used, the intent is not to exclude anyone. The intent is to simplify the wording employed.

If a sample refers to a particular person of known male gender, the male pronouns will be used. It is hoped that the terminology used will clarify rather than confuse.

INTRODUCTION

One of the definitions of graphology describes it as a scientific study and analysis of handwriting, or the art of interpreting character and personality from peculiarities in handwriting. This work will cover some of the basic factors of handwriting analysis for the explorer of graphology.

Handwriting is often called expressive, and indeed it is. All handwriting expresses the writer and her past. The experiences that are part of the past all make an impact on the writer. Some experiences make a deeper or more lasting impression than others. All that happens to a person is part of who they are. It is by interpreting how these past experiences affect the way one writes that gives graphologists insights into how a writer behaves.

Handwriting has also been called mind writing or brain writing. All that is part of the mind is reflected by an individual in many ways, writing being but one. We can attempt to disguise our feelings and thoughts, and often succeed to some extent, but to disguise ourselves totally is impossible. Given adequate samples, time, expertise, and purpose, there is very little that a writer can disguise from an expertly trained graphologist.

Many serious graphologists spend their entire lives studying, researching, and practicing this science. While this book is not intended to further educate already professional graphologists, it is hoped that it will assist those more recently involved in the study to begin quickly building a foundation and to make them aware how accurately they can interpret their own moods and traits.

Readers will develop new awareness as they observe their own and others' handwriting. However, much information that, for whatever reason, a person doesn't admit to self may continue to remain hidden as the writer selectively evaluates her writing.

I have divided some of the main factors into separate segments in this book. Each factor interacts with all of the other factors, but the divisions may make it easier if you first understand factors separately before combining them to arrive at a whole look.

Graphology is an exciting, useful tool, and some of the numerous ways of using it will be discussed later. It may open windows to many unexplored areas for the one who practices the skill, and I wish you success, delight, increasing awareness, and all good things in your pursuit of this subject.

Ruth Gardner

1

Some General Information

Brief History

The science of graphology has for many years been a tool to increase awareness of one's character or personality. Three thousand years ago Nero stated that he had no trust for an individual whose handwriting he thought showed him to be treacherous. Aristotle once wrote: "Spoken words are the symbols of mental experience, and written words are the symbols of spoken words. Just as men have not the same speech sounds, so all men have not the same writing."

Camillo Baldi, an Italian physician, in 1622 wrote the first book that we know of on graphology. The book was titled *How To Judge The Nature And The Character Of A Person From His Letter*. He commented on the fact that all writers write differently and that no one can write like another.

The word "graphology" was first used by Abby Michon of Paris. The word is taken from the Greek *graph*, meaning "writing" and *ology*, meaning "study." Michon collected and studied thousands of handwriting samples, and after many years published his system of analysis. He and/or his students established the Graphological Society in Paris, which was active until World War II intervened. A student of Michon's, Jean Cre'pieux-Jamin, emphasized that handwriting must be studied as a whole, as a gestalt, not as so many simple, unrelated characteristics. Each of us is a complicated creation with many characteristics of which we are the sum total. When those characteristics are in conflict they must be weighed one against the other to arrive at an accurate evaluation of the writing.

Ludwig Klages, a well-known German philosopher, established laws and principles of graphology during the late 1800s and early 1900s that are still used by many graphologists today. Klages' basic law of expression states that each expressive bodily movement actualizes the tensions and drives the personality. Klages also instituted the concept of "form level," which is judged by the general rhythm of a writing. (This concept is accepted or rejected depending on the graphologist's own desire and experience.) Among his many published books are *Handwriting and Character* and *The Problem of Graphology*.

Edgar Allan Poe analyzed handwriting and published some of his analyses. He used the word *autography* to describe his method of analysis. He stated that there are systemizable procedures to autography and that the analyst must be able to distinguish the differences between calculation and analysis. His observations and research were published in book form in 1926 by Dial Press of New York.

Gordon Allport, in his studies at Harvard Psychological Clinic in 1930, based his research on the assumption that (1) personality is consistent; (2) movement is expressive of personality; and (3) the gestures and other expressive movements of an individual are consistent with one another. Thus, he explained a basis for evaluating personality and how it is expressed in handwriting.

In 1955 Klara Roman and George Staemphli developed a checklist that organized certain factors and plotted them on a chart called a Graphological Psychogram. This psychogram was refined by Daniel Anthony of New York some years later.

For reasons unknown to me, the acceptance and practice of graphology in the United States has progressed more slowly than in other parts of the world, although there have been many noted American researchers. In Europe, psychologists have been leaders in the study of graphology, and psychology curriculums in many European universities require studies in handwriting psychology.

Some Specific Limits of Graphology

Before beginning the study of graphology, every student should be aware of some of the things graphology cannot tell the analyst about the writer. First and foremost, it cannot foretell the future. Many people equate graphology with some kind of extrasensory perception or clairvoyance. It is neither of these. As mentioned before, it is a scientific study. A graphologist may predict a writer's reaction to various situations, but this is not predicting the future. Should a graphologist accurately do predictions, she is using another skill, art, or practice to do so—not graphology.

A second factor, which the analyst usually does not even attempt to discern, is the exact age of the writer. One can often perceive the very old and the very young, but at times even this is difficult. Levels of maturity may be exposed by the writer, but that often has nothing to do with chronological age.

Gender of the writer is another fact that an analyst must guess at rather than be able to discern. Certain traits are often regarded, according to social values, as belonging to the male or the female; but with the recent trends toward changing these values and the acceptance of the individuality of each writer, this kind of evaluation is often invalid. A thorough analyst will require knowledge of age and sex before beginning an analysis.

Obtaining a Sample

When writing a sample or requesting one for analysis there are several simple rules that are important for an adequate sample:

1) Use unlined paper, at least six-by-nine inches and preferably larger —never a napkin, a grocery list, a post card, or a scrap of paper.

2) The writing implement should be the writer's usual pen, fountain or ballpoint, but not a pencil or a felt-tip pen.

3) Make sure the sample is at least one hundred words for a quick and simple analysis.

4) Do not use a sample that is copied from something already written and do not use poetry. The text is not important, but the writing seems to flow more accurately if it is thought about as the writer writes.

Having a variety of samples from the writer will also give you more information. Each sample is a reflection of the writer at the moment it is made. It will contribute additional information if you can see reflections from other times and other situations in the writer's life. You may want a sample from the past and one from a time when the writer was experiencing some particular emotional high or low, perhaps one from the previous week or one written yesterday. Any means toward building on the information available will assist in accuracy.

Cautions

Always remember that a trait observed is just one clue and must be combined with others to arrive at an accurate profile. Every trait is influenced by every other trait in handwriting, just as it is in life. Another fact important to remember is that the great majority of traits possess both positive and negative aspects and must be evaluated by considering all contributing factors.

A disciplined graphologist does not jump to conclusions on the basis of a few clues but evaluates the entire sample carefully, relying on many factors before making a judgment.

Beginning Examination

Your first contact with the writing and your first impressions are also very important. Don't concern yourself with individual words but look at it as a picture within a frame. Turn it sideways and upside down. Is it orderly, neat, messy, unbalanced, heavy? Are there other observations to substantiate your first impressions? Write down your first impressions and be aware of them as you proceed.

One of the hardest elements to evaluate, especially without a great deal of experience, is *form*. Is the form of the writing good form or bad, pleasant or unpleasant? Does it appear positive or negative? Is it fluid or rigid, natural or stilted? Consider the rhythm and harmony of the writing. Is it balanced? Do the contraction and release movements flow smoothly? Is there balance and symmetry present? Symmetry appears in the balance of the zones. Are the white spaces harmonious? Look at it as a whole rather than as individual strokes and spaces. Learning to judge form will assist you in selecting positive or negative traits from the lists throughout this book. Any excesses in handwriting are a means of compensating for what the writer sees, on some level, as a deficiency. How much of a compensation the writer needs is indicated by the degree of deficiency. The more excesses or the higher degrees of deficiency, the poorer the form the writing becomes.

It may be a good idea to begin looking at the bottom of the sample first, as the writer may be somewhat self-conscious at the beginning but forgets any anxiety as the writing proceeds.

The emotions that the writer felt upon writing the sample can often be discerned by repeating the strokes. Try making the same strokes or movements yourself as the writer did. See how it feels to you. Experiment with different pressures and different writing sizes, with back, forward and straight slants, with different sizes and lengths of lower zones of writing, and be aware of any changes that activity makes in your feelings. With practice this effort may lead to more awareness, not only of yourself but also of others.

Use of Transparencies

The transparencies included with this book will be referred to from time to time, and it is hoped that they will be of help for quicker and more accurate analysis. Placing the sample beneath the transparency will enable you to judge the evenness of the baseline, the slant of the letters, the distance between words and letters, consistencies, margin width and evenness, size, and many other helpful pieces of information.

2

Zone, Baseline, and Slant Factors

ZONES

UPPER . . . . intellectual or abstract
MIDDLE . . . . daily action or tangible
LOWER . . . . desire, drives, or biological

Three zones or portions of space above and below the writing line are used in handwriting analysis, and each is symbolic of the energy expended in that area of the writer's life.

All letters use the middle zone. The *b, d, h, i, k, l,* and *t* in lower case use the middle and upper zones. Lower-case *g, j, p, q, y,* and *z* occupy the middle and lower zones. The *f* is tri-zonal and the only lower-case letter that uses all three zones. All of the capital letters are bi-zonal and use the upper and middle zone, while the *J, Y,* and *Z* are tri-zonal.

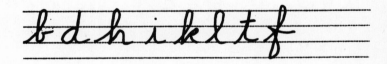

The habits used to place letters in the *upper zone* on the paper indicate the writer's behavior, feelings, and thoughts in areas of the spiritual, religious, political, and intangible. The concentration or emphasis, or lack of concentration or emphasis, shows how the writer addresses those areas of her life. Various extremes in this zone indicate departure from the ordinary in intangible and intellectual fields. An analyst may want to spend time studying this zone to understand how the writer acts, thinks, or feels about science, politics, spirituality, philosophy, imagination, creativity, and fantasy.

Large, full upper zones divulge a thoughtful person, probably with imagination and creativity but perhaps with an unrealistic self-image. The more flourished or enlarged or twirled, the more extreme the imagination and the more indicative of fantasy or daydreaming.

A writing unbalanced at the expense of this zone would indicate a lack of attention to, or consideration of, the intellectual or imaginative aspects.

Please fill in the

Since this sample has some originality and expressiveness, a fairly narrow, high, upper zone might indicate cautious thought but definite interest in thought and/or abstract matters.

I like being at this party.

A narrow upper zone reveals lack of imagination or creative thought if there is no originality or creativity shown elsewhere.

I'd paint myself.

The *middle zone* contains the letters that do not extend either up or down but remain flat on the imaginary or real line upon which the writing is based. The manner in which these letters are shaped and placed on the paper corresponds to the mundane realms of the writer's life—the daily action or tangible areas having to do with eating, sleeping, friendships, dressing, and like matters.

Middle-zone letters accentuated at the expense of the other zones indicate a particular interest in social relationships and conscious action at the expense of the material drives and desires and the intellectual aspects of life. A writer may be described as immature or insecure because of this imbalance. Frequently, the accentuation appears in the writing of young people in the process of maturing. They need to be particularly conscious of daily happenings and social relationships to identify with the process of maturing.

a c e m n o r s u v w x

instructors make me nervous.

A small, unaccentuated middle zone will probably be made up for by a concentration in one of the other zones, and this indicates that the concentration is paid for at the expense of the writer's daily life. It is probable that they are careless of the impressions they make and give no attention to expressing their own emotional needs.

look bad,
life is not

The *lower zone* corresponds to the basic drives of the writer. Money, possessions, physical exercise, and sex are some of the drives that may be investigated by attention to this zone.

The lower zone contains all bi-zonal letters extending below the baseline and the letter *f*, which is the only lower-case letter that is tri-zonal. Extremes in length may indicate extent of interest in biological drives and desires; extremes in pressure, the intensity of those desires; extremes in slant, the frequency of the need; and extremes in width, the amount of thought and/or speech involved. The lower zone is considered the area of the id, or the subconscious world of materialism and basic biological drives. Interests in sex and love, in sports and adventures, in instincts and drives, and in money and belongings are reflected here.

Full, long, and wide lower loops denote an active imagination and someone who is "on display," perhaps an actor or athlete and certainly a gregarious being. A need to hang on to money is also indicated by this sort of full, finished loop, particularly the *y*. This writer probably uses her great muscles, particularly the long thigh muscles to some extent. She certainly is involving her body in more than being a "couch potato."

Unusual lower loop formation denotes eccentricity or repression in the field of drives and desires, often in sex. Frequent unusual loops are often said to reveal unusual lovers, particularly if seen in the *g*. The same may be true of unusual attitudes or feelings regarding money or belongings if the *y* is unusual.

I am here to learn of myself
& my opportunity is to grow

Very long lower loops show much involvement, and if tangled into the lower line of writing the involvement is probably such that it is causing difficulty in the writer's life.

at Honeywell at
4 P.M. Don't

Angular bottom or lower loop formations may indicate uncompromising resentment, hostility, and perhaps difficulty in sexual gratification, whereas unclosed loops show frustration in the instinctive matters.

This day has been
too long
coming tommorrow.
to go home, but
nd staying longer.

A stroke in any area that suddenly stops and changes direction or is angular indicates stress or irresolution in that area of the writer's life.

Everything

No loops whatsoever may represent materialistic and sexual repression.

Hi, my name is

I am very anxious

Individuals often omit loops if the letter is the last in a word, but usually loops can be found in loop letters falling in the middle of a word. A firm single stroke down is also a sign of firmness in the writer, and if the ending is firm and abrupt, of possible supervisory ability, of definiteness.

from the strength gained
of day and the darkness

Very short lower loops show unimportance of basic drives, or materialism. They may particularly indicate an absence of physical exercise or involvement. There are probably concentrations in one of the other zones.

write something for you?

As mentioned earlier, the lower-case *f* is the only lower-case letter that occupies all three zones. A well-balanced, centrally placed *f* denotes just that in the writer. Balance and organizational ability come easily to such a person.

profession

An overinflated bottom loop on the *f* seems to indicate an interest in food. The writer may be a dieter, a gourmet cook, a teacher of cooking, or just someone who loves to eat.

The psychic fair is having a fabulous turnout. Sorry, but I

Consider how you, the reader, feel when making certain types of strokes into the various zones. Check your zones when a rare mood affects you or when a new and changing experience has occurred. Practice being aware of your own feelings and how you express them on paper. An emphasis in one zone must detract from the other two, and very rarely are all three zones consistently balanced. How do you feel when you balance them? How do you feel when you don't?

BASELINE SLANT

The slant of the baseline—the imaginary line on which the bottoms of the middle zone letters align—denotes pessimistic or optimistic tendencies better than any other factor. Check your own writing when feeling depressed or discouraged. Unless you have a great deal of control the lines may descend. Do you feel loved and accomplished, healthy and invigorated? Chances are pretty good that your writing ascends at a time like this. These climbing or falling tendencies may be temporary or they can be an indication of your general feelings about life.

Check a sample using the transparent grid. Place the grid over the sample and you have an instant guide to the positions of a baseline.

To get a good view of the baseline of writing, turn the sample to the side and look at it as a line instead of as a baseline of writing. Look at it from both margins while holding it sideways.

The direction of the baseline may be dependent on a temporary condition, such as a mental state or physical condition. In order to take account of this factor for an accurate analysis, the analyst needs several different samples written at different times.

When the baseline of writing slants up to the right, one or more of the following may be indicated:

optimism

faith in the future

feeling of being loved

excitement

joy

invigoration

When the baseline slants down to the right these feelings are a possibility:

pessimism

fatigue

discouragement

depression

illness

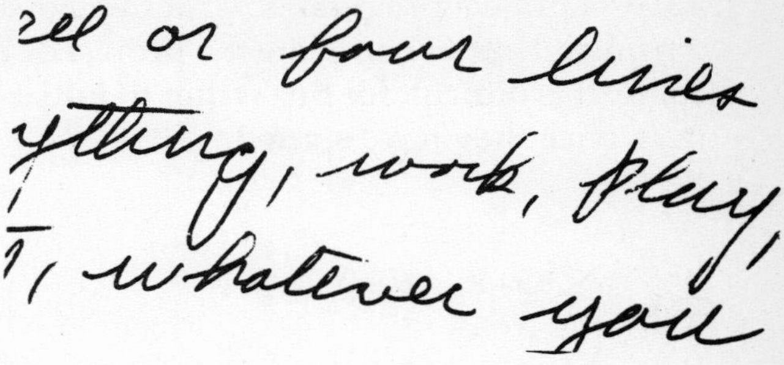

[handwritten sample]

If the baseline is parallel to the top and bottom of the paper, the following characteristics are suggested:

reliability

even temper

control of emotions

reason rules

unwavering resolution

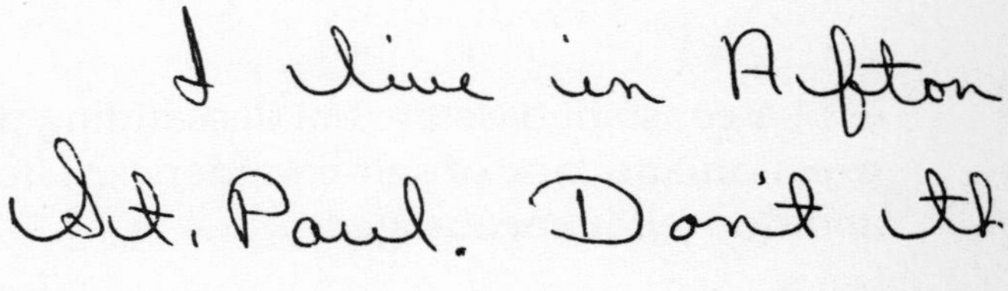

[handwritten sample]

Occasionally you will see a baseline so straight it will appear as though the writer wrote above a ruler. This implies that the writer needs control, very strong control, in her life in order to be comfortable.

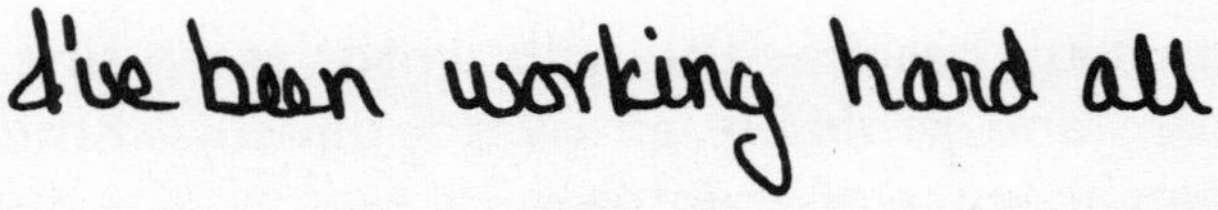

[handwritten sample]

If the baseline forms an arc, writer begins a project or an interest with enthusiasm and optimism but tires of it and gives up, and probably doesn't finish a lot of the projects that are started. This writer would do well in a position where she initiates projects rather than follows them all the way through.

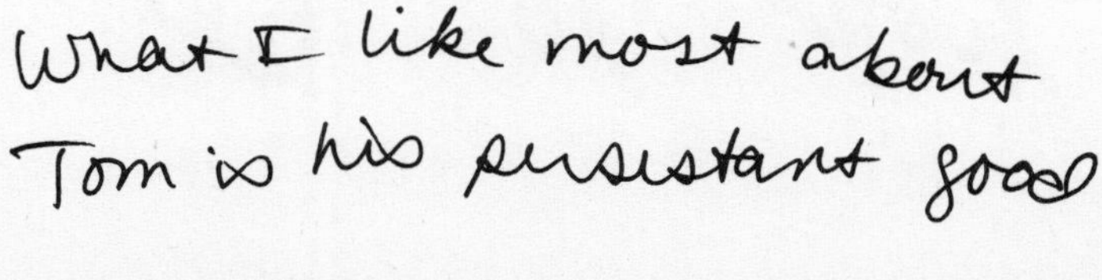

[handwritten sample]

If the baseline forms a dish or concave, the writer is a slow starter without a lot of confidence or purpose, perhaps due to bad breaks or health; but as a project progresses, writer will overcome much of beginning negativism and either complete the project or become optimistic about the outcome. It is difficult for this writer to initiate projects but easier to take them over once they have started.

If you're not a part of the Solution than you're a part of the problem

A constant baseline but descending words indicates a fight against depression and lack of self-confidence. These writers need encouragement and do well if encouraged.

give you my hand

A constant baseline but with words ascending reveals the writer has enthusiasm and probably an overoptimistic attitude toward life. It also denotes an absence of stamina.

hope to be

LETTER SLANT

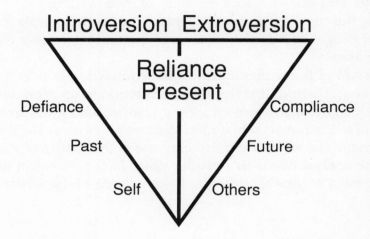

This diagram shows how some traits correspond to the various degrees of letter slant. Letter slant has to do with the writer's emotional direction and degree of emotional control. About 77 percent of writers write with a right slant, 15 percent with a left slant, and the remaining 8 percent write vertically.

Certain obvious characteristics can usually be inferred from the slant of the writing, which is always symbolic. The writer whose writing leans forward (to the right) does just that emotionally. A right-slanted writer leans toward friendships, the future, toward compliance and extroversion. The left-slanted writer leans back to the past and away from people, toward introversion and self. The left-slanted may isolate themselves more than the right-slanted writers, but since their lives aren't so intertwined with others, there may be more time and energy for creative pursuits.

As mentioned earlier, none of these factors stand alone. A left-slanted writer may have other strong characteristics in her writing that diminish the above stated meaning of a left slant. For instance, as you will read later, words with narrow spaces between them show that the writer does not want space between herself and others. Also, a page of writing without margins indicates the writer wants to be close to others. The analyst must look at more than one characteristic to arrive at an evaluation.

When making notes during a routine telephone call or writing a grocery list, a writer may write in a vertical slant; on the other hand, while writing a letter to a lover the writing may have a sharp right slant. The emotions of the writer are reflected in the slant of the writing. Many writers will inform you that they write in different ways. Of course they do. Their emotional involvement varies and often so does the slant of their writing.

Using the curved transparency, place it over the sample for an instant emotional gauge. Be sure the baseline of the sample follows the bottom of the transparency.

The slant of the letters indicates the connection between the writer's inner and outer world. It is the writer's reaction to environmental factors. You may imagine a writer with a right slant reaching out to the right, to others, and to the future, while a left slant would portray the opposite. The more extreme the slant, the more extreme is the nature of the writer. Of course, the analyst needs to consider other factors to select which of the following traits accurately describe the emotions of the writer.

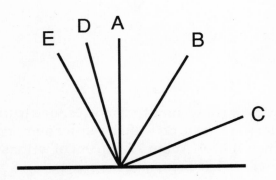

This diagram is lettered to assist in following the categories below.

A. Vertical slant:
   head controls the heart
   matter-of-fact personality
   independent emotional nature
   oriented to work well alone
   lack of spontaneity
   ability to control emotions in
   crises

B. Moderate right slant:
    ability to express opinions
    confidence in convictions
    freedom of thought
    extroverted
    future orientation
    demonstrative and expressive
    affectionate and kind
    impulsive to minor degree

C. Extreme right slant:
    lack of self-control
    impulsive
    unrestrained
    intense and involved
    very expressive
    supersensitive (possibly
      radical)
    dependent on others
    little resistance to im-
      pressions
    low frustration tolerance

D. Moderate left slant:
    reflective
    independent
    objective
    nonsympathetic
    difficulty in expressing
      emotions
    self-contained
    possible repression and
      inhibition
    difficulty in adapting
    choosiness about color,
      designs, materials and
      things concerning self,
      such as clothes, car,
      and friends

E. Extreme left slant:
    repressed childhood
    early rejection
    fear of the future
    possible evading of
      reality
    apprehensive of
      intimacy
    defensive

F. Irregular slant:
    extreme sensitivity
    moodiness
    unpredictability
    versatility
    ambivalence

In regard to the irregular slant described above, note that this type of writer does not know how to approach relationships. Sometimes she reaches out and sometimes she holds back and is unpredictable as to how she will react to others. The symbology is very apparent, as these letters sometimes lean toward others (to the right) and sometimes lean away (to the left).

3

Size and Pressure Factors

SIZE

The variations in size and size factors are almost infinite. For reasons of simplicity and space this work will cover only the main ones:

tall
small
narrow
broad

Size is the writer's projection of self-importance. The writing size usually indicates the size the writer claims among other people. It is a measure of self-esteem. If all uni-zonal letters are less than three millimeters in height, the writing is considered small. To be evenly balanced the bi-zonal letters should be once again the size of the uni-zonal letters. Three millimeters is pretty average size. The grid transparency is measured off in three-millimeter increments and can be used to help judge writing size.

The width of a letter is judged by the vertical size. In a uni-zonal letter such as *a*, if the distance between the downstrokes is equal to the height, the letter is judged to be of medium width. If the distance is greater, it is judged to be broad, and if less, narrow.

Again, the characteristics assigned to various sizes of writing are just one clue and need to be combined with other clues to arrive at an accurate evaluation.

The height reflects the writer's working for stature and prestige.

(handwriting sample)

Tall

importance of approval to the
  writer
ambition
observation of things in general
farsightedness
lack of objectivity
lack of consideration
lack of modesty
lack of tact

(handwriting sample)

Small

writer looks at life through microscope
analytical nature
modesty and reserve
ability to concentrate
unconcerned with own image
resourcefulness
thriftiness
lack of self-confidence
obedience
accurate individual
observant
conservative concerning money
  and time
meticulous worker

Width of writing indicates the amount of living space or elbow room the writer needs and often demands.

Broad or wide

desire for travel
need to spend on self
fantasizing nature
boastful nature
self-assurance
egotism
indiscretion
pride
lack of concentration
tolerance
lack of discipline and tact
natural approach
frankness
friendliness
imaginative
artistic
spontaneous
broadminded
sociable

way to spend afternoon. I warm up and

Lincoln P. O Lucasvi

Extremely wide

obtrusive
impudent
intrusive

Graphologist. lectures, & grou instruction

Being asked to write is a privilege

Thank

Narrow:

restriction
conservatism
inhibition
self-discipline
economical nature
concentration ability
distrustful nature
socially passive nature
self-control and moderation
contracting or witholding nature
critical
inartistic
introverted
timid
seclusive
suspicious

Big single-zone letters are often a sign of immaturity or that the writer has a limited amount of education. As writers mature and become more adept at coordinating small muscle movement, the loops become longer and the middle zone more in proportion.

irregular the more of the US in flocks

Big uni-zonals

desire for greatness
hero worship
fondness for food
eccentricity

Irregular size

moodiness
vivaciousness
quick temper
excitable
unpredictable

off the clock paed

Capital Letter Size

Tall and narrow

shyness and pride
coolness
inhibited
reserved
dignified
sober

Mary Mc.

Tall and exaggerated

imagination
ambition
artistic talent
braggart
compensation for inferiority
   complex
farsighted
visionary
proud
independent
haughty

Small

realist
provincial
materialistic
docile
meticulous worker
collector of facts
modest
objective
concentrates on facts, not ideas

Tapering down to the right

diplomacy
condescension
patronizing

Tapering up to the right

outward confidence
inner subordination
immaturity and childishness
self-consciousness

The greater the elaboration, the more feelings of actual superiority or the greater the compensatory reaction to inferior feelings.

Unnecessary capitals within
sentences

need to stand out
need to be noticed
ostentation

PRESSURE

Pressure is the graphologist's measure of the writer's vitality, intensity, or determination. The amount of pressure used is not a conscious habit and usually not done with the writer's awareness. Pressure shows the force or lack of force of the writer's personality. Generally, downstrokes are somewhat heavier and upstrokes are somewhat lighter than the rest of the writing.

A feeling of dominance or intensity will produce a heavier pressure than feelings of sympathy and caring. Practice writing with a heavy pressure and notice your feelings as opposed to when you write with very light pressure. Then run your fingers over both sides of the paper at once and feel the lines as they have come through or not come through the paper. With this method the fingers can detect pressure that the eye cannot see.

A writer with heavy pressure indicates a deeply intense personality, a strong vitality, and probably one with strong determination. Such a writer soaks up emotional experiences and retains the impression made by these experiences for long periods of time.

Extremely heavy pressure reveals poorly channeled energy, as exhibited by a beginning writer and those who are vain, ill, or secretive. If this pressure is combined with slow writing, it may indicate an inhibition without outlets, a depression and/or frustration.

Heavy pressure

creative power
strong libido
dominance
enthusiasm
involvement
endurance
emotional strength
deep commitments
lasting memory of wrongs
sensuousness
desire for physical expression
preference for dark or bright
  colors
holds grudges

Light pressure can be observed by thin lines that have made no impression on the reverse side of the paper and by a very light color to the written lines.

Light pressure

little intensity, vitality, or
  determination
sensitive nature
forgives rapidly
tenderness
desire to avoid friction
resists commitment
spirituality
physical weakness
preference for pastel colors
adaptability
passive indifference

If pressure is *displaced*, or the rhythm of slightly heavier pressure on the downstroke and lighter pressure on the upstroke is changed or unusual, the trait expressed may be unresolved anger—either conscious or unconscious. It may indicate the writer feels hostility in the environment. Sudden unrhythmic changes in pressure are always a negative trait indication.

Displaced pressure

inner conflicts
inferiority complex
moodiness
unsteady will power
emotional instability

lake

If pressure is absent on left-descending upper-zone strokes, a fear of the past is implied.

Cooking

If pressure is absent on right-ascending upper-zone strokes, one may suspect fear of the future.

a man

Sudden pressure changes such as club-ending T bars or other club endings (blunt, firm strokes) may reveal sudden emotional intensity or a quick temper.

Pastosity in writing, which is recognized by the evidence of extra ink in various places in the writing, is due to displaced pressure. In the days of quill pens and even fountain pens it was easy to recognize. Now with ballpoint and felt-tip pens the graphologist must stretch a little harder. Extra ink is left by the force with which the writer uses the pen. In using a felt-tip the line may spread just a little more, and even a ballpoint may look a little wider. In writing that has healthy, harmoniously changing pressure, the line will appear to have a noticeable rhythm to the variations in pressure. In a negative pastose writing the writers do not follow any discernible rhythm but displace pressure in very unharmoniously placed lumps.

Rhythmic changing pressure

aesthetic, artistic nature
perceptiveness
unrestrained natural personality
pleasure in sense gratification
warm, colorful, charming personality

Blotchy, messy, filled-in, untidy strokes often indicate unresolved and perhaps misunderstood sensual interests. The writing is often very difficult to read.

Unrhythmic, discordant changing pressure

lack of self-discipline
undependability
maladjustment to life
possible erratic temperament
concealing nature

4

Stroke Factors

CONNECTING STROKES

There are four main kinds of connecting strokes, and although writers often use one of them more often than another, most use a combination. Connecting strokes show the attitude of the writer toward others.

Garland is a rounded, cup-like stroke and the connecting form generally taught to students in western schools. The garland is the quickest, easiest, most natural connection to make. However, as the student matures the form may change or it may remain the same, depending on the personality of the writer. It is a gesture of release that suggests receptivity, an openness to all influences. The deeper the garland, or "cup," the more receptive the writer. Imagine the cup of the writer being filled by another. The more space in the cup, the more room for the writer to receive.

Moderate garland

desire to avoid conflict
adaptable
kind and sympathetic
outgoing
appears extroverted
good listener
uncalculating
hospitable
talkative
flexible
indolent
receptive
careless
thoughtless
lazy

Deep garland

depressiveness
deep sympathy for the helpless
contemplative
takes on another's pain

Shallow garland

reckless
superficial
lacks restraint
elusive
obliging manners
amiable

Arcade connection is the most artistic but is unnatural and a very slow form. It is often chosen by the writer who feels she requires protection. The arcade writer also seems to feel a need to retreat from the world to contemplate or consider. Imagine the stroke as an umbrella or an arm elevated over the head to protect and shield. The more arched the stroke, the more artistic and protective the writer. The more shallow, the more the writer places a lid on things or covers up something. Generally, the flatter the arcade, the more negative evaluation the graphologist can give it.

Arcade

artistic builder
protective
places importance on
　appearance rather than
　on essence
lacks spontaneity
shyness
reserve
meditativeness
good manners
formal
poise
pride
individualistic

Flat arcade

schemer
hypocrite
pretentious
secretive
defensive

Angular form is a representation of a most highly controlled contraction and release. The arcade writer is goal-oriented, pursuing achievement of tasks. To form this very slow stroke the writer must stop and deliberately change direction, which indicates a stress or irresolution or discomfort. Such a writer is driven or forced by some past programming into this mode.

Angular

tense
excitable
goal-oriented
competitive
aggressive
decisive
logical
cold-blooded
strict
disciplined
dissatisfied
slow and thorough
intolerant
persistent
idealistic
initiating

Thread is a composite connective form showing the writer's commitment to self. The thread writer has an intuitive capacity for attaining temporary identification with the feelings of others but more as a chameleon than with empathy. They are clever but not at the expense of others, and work without making waves. They have a dislike of being categorized. If a graphologist were to assess the most difficult samples to obtain, it would probably be that of a thread writer. Such writers seldom request analysis, although if put in the position of having to refuse, they may not do so because their unwillingness to stand up and fight often prevents them from refusing.

Legible thread with pressure

perceptive
insightful
versatile
entrepreneur
statesmanlike
usually very intelligent
does the "right" thing
yielding

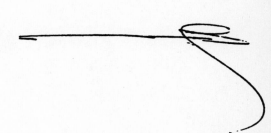

Thread without pressure

indecisive
cunning
perceptive
yielding
insightful

In addition to the above connections, the presence or absence of a connecting stroke is also important.

Connected writing in good form without breaks between words or letters

logical thinking
steady flow of thought
adaptation to environment
tenacity and persistence
cooperative
lack of initiative
dependent

this psychic fair

Unconnected first letter

pause before beginning
observant (pauses to look)
may dislike deciding
cautious
procrastinator

friends

Unconnected last letter

pause after well into project but
    before really committed
hesitant nature
reconsiders decisions
ambivalence

Disconnectedness is a gesture of isolation, of enclosure, and it may lead to attractive new wholes or to withdrawal. The evaluation of writing with disconnections between letters within the same word is so complicated and involved that I choose not to go into it here. An excellent book, *Handwriting, A Key to Personality* by Klara G. Roman, is available should you choose to further investigate this subject.

BEGINNING STROKES

Beginning strokes disclose the manner in which the writer grasps new situations or the calculated impression the writer makes; they announce the way the writer adjusts to a new job or assesses new situations; and they show the writer's intentions and the importance of the past.

Long and curved

mannerly
needs time to prepare for activities
obedient, comfortable with the
   past
fussy about details
likes formalisms

Unbending

"chip on the shoulder"
has known imposition
tensions from the past
resentment
lacks assurance
lacks confidence
resistant to change

to see

Long, below baseline stroke

subconscious drive to succeed
impatient and aggressive in
   preparation
argumentative

are what you are. The mis

Curved right to left

collector
desire to own or save
possessive

the

Hooked under

jealously acquisitive

Errol Flynn

Long underlining

self-admiration
self-importance
compensation for inferiority
   complex

Of my favorit

of the year

Starting in upper zone

idealistic
enterprising
religious awareness

The fact that

giggles just

pink. Here is

Absent

desire to begin without delay
dislikes waste of time and energy
objective
practical
intelligent
not superficial

The longer the beginning stroke, the more important the past remains and the more firmly attached the writer to that past.

ENDING STROKES

Ending strokes show social attitude. They show a writer as he or she really is (as opposed to the appearance given) and the social manners or current behavior of the writer. These final strokes divulge the adaptability of the writer to the environment, the writing speed of the writer, and her attitudes based on past experience. They show the real nature and unconscious acts.

Long, blunt, outward- and upward-tending

genuine giver
generous
outgoing

Upward-tending tapered

reluctant giver
expects reward from giving
"strings" attached to gift

High-reaching

search for knowledge
unusual or mysterious interest

Blunt, extended, club-like

cruel and/or brutal
firm and unyielding

Blunt unextended

frankness and bluntness
decisive concerning self

Sharp, below baseline

argumentative
cruel
obstinate

Final reaching back to left

introversion
self-protectiveness
self-interest
insecurity

Missing

abrupt and unobliging
reserved
reticent
honest, discriminating mind
confidence in own resources
self-discipline
shyness
compulsiveness
selfishness

Extended

possessive
cautious

Unfinished

doesn't finish projects
selfish
procrastinates

Coverstroke

screens thoughts and actions
secretive

Hook left and down

grasping
greedy

done!

Final pulled down and under

selfish
concentrated self-interest
often loses temper

gools

Burst of pressure

easily loses temper
unbearable emotions

and seven

Long tapered whip

quick to lose temper

meeting

5

Spacing Factors

LETTER SPACING

The amount of space between letters indicates the extent to which the writer relies upon cooperation with others or on her own intuition. The size of the space is a nondeliberate act. As in each of the factors studied, be aware that each factor supplies only a clue to the total picture of the writer and must be assessed along with other factors.

Close-spaced letters

tight
crowded
repressed
inhibited
scared
selfish
hostile
resentful

I m hear
r from you
'ose for wor

Wide-spaced letters

extroverted
sympathetic and understanding
squanders own resources

WORD SPACING

Space between words in writing is nondeliberate, just as spacing between words in speech usually is. A writer's words follow one another in the same way they do in her speech. Listening to a writer talk will tell you about the spacing between the words she writes. Symbolically, the space between words shows the degree of contact the writer establishes with her immediate environment. The grid transparency will be helpful in judging the evenness of the spacing. Space between words usually takes up the same space as a middle-zone, lower-case *a* at the beginning or the end of a word.

on the phone this r
coincidence we dis
interesting, and all

Even spaces

ease with people
reasonableness
self-confidence
good balance
acceptance
unadventurousness

This is such a r
spend a Sund
r truly having a

Uneven spaces

changeable social attitudes
insecure
gullible
possible thought hesitation
communication difficulty
spontaneity

Small spaces show desire to maintain close or constant interrelations with others.

Small spaces

extroversion
talkativeness
impulsiveness
insecurity
spontaneous

Large spaces show a need for elbow room, for solitude.

Large spaces

critical and cautious nature
philosophical
cultured
introverted
perhaps opinionated
inhibited or shy
isolationist
extravagant

Very large spaces

wastes paper and
   others' time
egotistical and
   inconsiderate
marked isolationist

LINE SPACING

Spacing between lines seems to be deliberately planned and signifies a picture of the organization of a writer's mind. It is a reflection of the writer's sense of direction, concern for order, and valuation of time.

consider myself. s
I hope it's a good
I look forward

Even line spacing:

system and planning
unadventurous
consistent

the darling
next store
first of all

Wide line spacing

objectivity
aloneness
mental agility
good manners
organization
self-assurance
lack of spontaneity

that will
that is, is

Narrow line spacing

thriftiness
hasty decision-making
lack of reserve
spontaneous
frugal

Very wide spacing

aloneness
desire for noninvolvement
possible separation from
   reality

Overlap, tangling with line below

lack of inhibition
overinvolvement with
   activities
preoccupation with
   instincts

6

Margins

Margins are an accurate measuring factor only if on a full sheet of paper. As in each factor studied, check your own margins at various times in your life.

Margins show the writer's degree of economy, consistency, tolerance, desire for esteem, and urge for acceptance. Margins reveal the place the writer desires to occupy and that which she does occupy. The left, upper, and lower margins are deliberately chosen, while the right is only occasionally chosen. Well-spaced margins signify an intelligent arrangement of time and space accompanied by favorable organization.

Upper and lower margins in correspondence—The upper margin is said to address the degree of esteem the writer has for the receiver.

Wide upper	*Wide lower*
formality	superficiality
reserve	aloofness
modesty	idealism
esteem for reader	sexual or emotional
withdrawal	trauma

Narrow upper

informality
directness
lack of respect for
    reader

Narrow lower

depression
fatigue
sensuousness

Left margins indicate the expectation of and desire for esteem or the space we wish to maintain between self and others. They also reveal the economic tendencies of the writer.

Right margins show the distance the writer actually keeps between self and others.

Widening
left margin

impatience
haste
enthusiasm
impulsiveness
lavishness
waning thriftiness
eager for contact
    with others

Narrowing
right margin

decreasing shyness

Narrowing
left margin

shyness
unsociable initially
progressive closeness
depression
unmanageable sense of
    thrift
illness
lack of spontaneity

Irregular
right margin

unwise thriftiness
love of travel
ambivalent social
    attitude

Even left margin

self-discipline
good manners

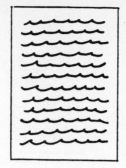

Even right margin

intolerance
conformity to set
standards
rigidity
anxious and
self-conscious

Wide left margin

self-respect
high standards
cultural background
desired distance
   from others
shyness
late riser

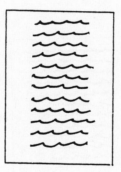

Wide right margin

fear of future
oversensitiveness
unrealistic
poor mixer, aloof
extravagance
fastidiousness
reserved
self-conscious
wasteful

*Extremely wide
left margin*

flight from self
very reserved
snobbish
unhappy childhood
often divorced
pathological shyness
courage and sociability

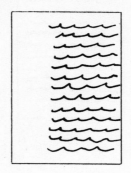

Narrow right margin

seeks close relationships
deep urge for acceptance
loquacity
gregariousness
joiner and mixer
impulsiveness

Narrow left margin

familiarity
desire for popularity
thriftiness or desire
   to receive due
free and easy manner
economical and practical
interest in others
early riser

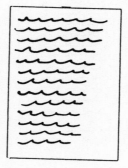

Widening right margin

fear of others
withdrawal

Narrow, absent on all sides

stinginess
acquisitiveness
morbid curiosity
tactlessness
obtrusiveness
unlimited sympathy

kindness
charity
fondness for luxury
hospitality

Wide all sides

aesthetic
lonely
withdrawn

aloofness
spiritual independence
secrecy about self

Irregular all sides

versatility
tolerance
disorganization

carelessness
inattentiveness

7

Self-Image

PERSONAL PRONOUN

In doing a quick, superficial analysis in which the writer wants to know about her complete personality in five minutes, the most important parts of the sample are the signature and the personal pronoun *I*. In a more lengthy and professional analysis, samples of these areas are also very important.

The pronoun *I* is the only letter, at least in the English language, that refers solely to the writer. One letter, the ego-symbol capital *I*, is a reflection of the writer and of all of the past that she has lived through.

That past begins when the soul enters the body and that entity begins the life journey. All that happens from that time onward will affect and leave an imprint on the psyche. From the very beginning the impressions made on the being become part of the personality.

The first contact with another person is the baby's contact with the mother. Corresponding to the mother figure is that first upward stroke of the capital *I*. That first loop shows the influence of the mother on the child as she teaches through example, whether she is aware of it or not. The lessons she teaches are many, but among them she teaches what the feminine is, how a female behaves, and consequently what the child can expect from the female. The second loop shows the influence of the father as he models and teaches the masculine, how a male behaves, and what can be expected from the male.

The gentle curves of a copybook "mother loop," or first loop, symbolize the female influence. In addition to showing how the writer was influenced by the mother, this stroke, by virtue of its presence in the upper zone, also reveals the height of the ego.

The second, or "father" loop shows the influence of the father by its length. The force of the straight line driving to the right, or future, denotes some of the "male" force the writer feels concerning herself.

The printed personal pronoun *I* also conveys information regarding the male and female images of the writer. The top stroke corresponds to the first loop in cursive writing as the mother stroke. A longer and/or heavier top stroke gives much the same information that the first loop does: The mother has left more of an impression on the writer than the father.

By the same token, if the bottom stroke is longer and/or heavier, then the father has had more influence. The size and pressure factors remain the same.

When the stroke is single and unadorned, the writer may see self as standing alone, independent. The behavior will certainly reflect that image of independence.

However, should that single stroke be bowed in one direction or the other, the writer, although wanting to be independent and self-sufficient, probably has not accomplished this desire. A bow to the right indicates pressure from the left, or from the mother, and may indicate difficulty in the writer's femaleness. This applies to both male and female writers. In a woman there might be fear of motherhood or feelings of inadequacy as a woman. In a man the fears might relate to his gentle side, to his ability to show concern and caring.

A single stroke bowed to the left because of pressure from the right would be a clue to difficulty in the writer's maleness and the expression and acceptance of such.

This writer has a strong ego-image when you compare the height of the personal pronoun *I* to the rest of the writing. This is borne out by the firm pressure and good form of the writing. She also was more influenced, positively or negatively, by her mother. Looking at the father loop, one sees a very sharp change of direction rather than the easier change of the copybook style, which as in any such stroke is a sudden stop and change of direction showing stress. The lack of follow-through in the final movement to the right perhaps shows something unresolved in her relationship with her father, and by the same token, a less than favorable image of the male parts of herself and perhaps even of men in general.

This second sample also shows a strong ego-image because of the height of the letter, but this writer was much more influenced by her father. Notice the size of the father loop and the pressure.

A complete absence of father is noted in the next sample. The absence may indicate exactly that—that the writer was raised solely by his mother, perhaps due to divorce or death. Or it is possible that it may mean that his father was a truck driver and not in the home very much. It is, however, more likely that the father was totally absent. The sharp point on the mother loop signifies a sharp, curious mind and perhaps some resentment or stress in the relationship with mother.

Separation of parents is often shown by the symbolic separation of the two strokes. If the pair were not separated in reality, then the child saw them as separate. The combined strength of a team was not present in the child's eyes. Such is the case with this writing sample. Although the *I* is pulled down into the lower zone, it is of adequate size to reveal a good ego-image. Its presence in the lower zone may indicate the importance of perception through the physical senses. Perhaps there is a concern about power or love as shown through the physical.

This upper-level manager was very much influenced by his father. Again, the pointed upper stroke shows a sharp, curious mind, but the mother's influence is squeezed out as the stroke retraces the original stroke.

A first loop so enlarged is often called a "smothering mother" loop. It is probable that this writer's mother did just that to her. It is safe to say that decisions were often made by the mother, perhaps without even consulting the child and probably for many years past childhood.

The symbol shown here has similarities with a treble clef in music, giving a clue to the writer's liking of music. The rhythm present may also indicate that she has musical ability. The final stroke is stronger than the first but remains unfinished. This is one indication of the lack of "male" follow-through in the writer. The final stroke also resembles the "rocking chair I," which indicates the writer has accepted the father, although the father doesn't live up to the image that the writer expected of him.

The sharp peak on the first loop indicates a very sharp mind with perhaps a bit more influence by the mother, although the father loop is full, which may somewhat balance it. The upright position of the *I* when compared to the right slant of the rest of the writing indicates that the writer is somewhat of a loner, being able to stand alone, although he is friendly and reaches out to others. He doesn't need others to the extent that most do, which is revealed by both the straight-standing *I* and the fairly wide spacing of his words.

This *I* has some similarity to a star, which indicates the writer's "high" aspirations. His follow-through stroke does follow through, although it fades out to a sharp point, revealing that he gives up before reaching his goal. This is supported by a number of unfinished final strokes elsewhere in his writing. The pressure is strong and the size appropriate, although the rest of the writing is in poor form. This, along with the reversed mother and father loops, shows difficulty in the ego of the writer, who has turned away from both parents, probably with good cause.

Another middle-management male entirely eliminates his mother loop and leaves a stark, sharp stroke in her place. His father loop reverses the swing back to the right, or the future. Although he probably identifies more strongly with his father, the reversing of the final stroke indicates he has turned away from him also. The writing is quite angular, with fairly heavy pressure and only a slight right slant, which probably indicates a strong, aggressive personality driven by a need to be independent and self-sufficient.

This small and almost insignificant little baby *I* conveys that the writer feels these same things about herself. The mother stroke is prominent and the integration area where the two loops come together is smeared. This smearing in that area is repeated throughout the sample. Although she saw her parents as a team, it probably wasn't a very clean, supportive team. In some areas of the sample the *I* leans very far to the right, suggesting that she thinks of herself first. Perhaps she had to, since her support system wasn't very evident in her beginnings.

This printed personal pronoun has a long, overhanging top stroke, which attests to the influence of the mother. The size is small when compared to the other letters and shows a poor or small ego-image.

This is just a small sampling of the characteristics the personal pronoun *I* reveals, and as in all of graphology, the graphologist must combine the above-described traits with others in order for them to have validity. The more support there is for a revealed trait, the more sure you can be that the trait is present in the personality. If seen only occasionally, then the trait is only an occasional one in the writer.

A book that covers the personal pronoun *I* in detail and is a must for any graphologist is *You and Your Private I* by Jane Green. It is listed in the Bibliography.

SIGNATURES

A signature is the writer's calling card. It is the image she projects to the outer world. It is a trademark of the writer. A signature is an offering of the way the writer *wants* the world to see her. It is not necessarily the way she is. This is particularly evident if the signature style differs from the main body of the writing. A signature is deliberate, whereas much of the writing, especially the personal pronoun, is undeliberate.

Many writers practice with various signatures, particularly in their teenage years, until they find one that seems to fit them. The signature often will change as their circumstances and needs change.

How the writer feels about her family, particularly her parents, is often evident in her signature.

Anais Nin seldom used her full name, which signified that her own personal title superseded in importance her family name and hence her family. The signature has the same pressure, the same slant, and the same size as her writing, indicating a fairly healthy integration between her personal and public self.

There is a possibility that the following lines and signatures were enlarged, but it is not certain. This is one of the many disadvantages of dealing with photocopies as a sample. Notice the large capital letters in President Carter's signature as compared with the body of the writing. This might indicate a discrepancy between his inner and outer confidence, or the position he wanted people to see he held as opposed to his personal modest assessment of himself. The slant of both the signature and the body of the writing seems similar, which reveals that he is comfortable with the way he projects warmth in both his personal and public lives. Again, with a photocopy it is difficult to discern pressure, but since it appears to be written with a felt-tip pen and is not noticeably different in width, we can assume that the pressure is similar, which shows a healthy balance of physical and psychic energy.

While we do not have a sample of the rest of her writing, Rosalynn Carter's signature has a larger capital letter to her first name than to her second, which suggests an emphasis on her personal goals and strengths rather than dependence on her husband for support. It may also indicate that her mother was the authority figure in her family.

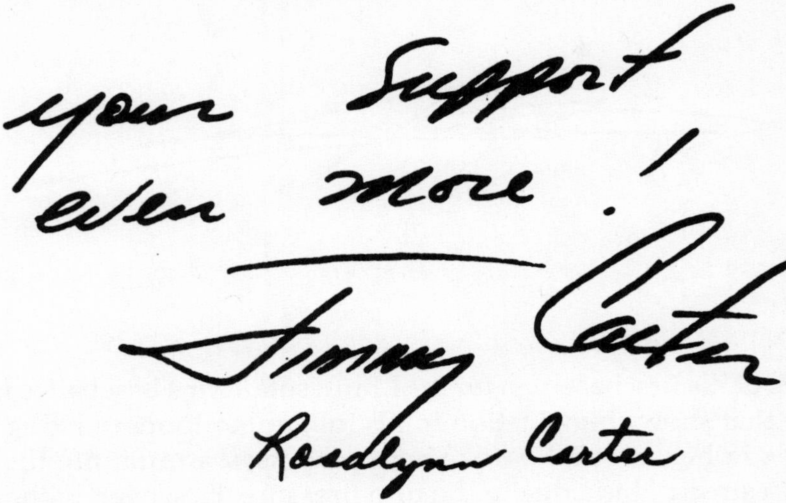

[handwritten signature: "your support even more! Jimmy Carter" with "Rosalynn Carter" below]

The following signature is also a photocopy, and there is no further writing for comparison. It was signed to the letter in which Richard Nixon tendered his resignation as President of the United States. The poor form is probably a result of the emotional stress in this biggest crisis of his life. His first-name capital letter is much larger than his last, indicating his pride in his accomplishments and feeling of separation from his family of birth, and it is probable that his mother was also the authority figure in his family. Note the hook on the *x* pulled down into the lower zone and the badly formed capital *R*.

[handwritten signature: "Richard Nixon"]

Slashing through a signature is as symbolic as it looks. It probably is a slashing of self, a crossing out of self. If less definite but nevertheless an obliteration, it probably shows a need to not be known, to be covered or disguised, to be secret about one's self.

Kent Hrbek, a first baseman for the Minnesota Twins baseball team, has a signature that shows imagination in his full, upper loops; a liking of the opposite sex in his second *K* stroke wrapping itself around the first stem stroke; and a strong libido due to the firm pressure. However, without any additional writing, all we know is that this is how he wants to be viewed.

Carolyn Dodson, a noted author and astrologist, signs her first name much larger, in height as well as width, which suggests that rather than leaning on her husband, she has pride in self and wants others to see it. The rest of her signature and the body of her writing have a similar pressure, size, slant, and speed, attesting to her health in most areas.

Gene Larkin, another Minnesota Twins player, shows family pride with his taller capital *L* in his last name. If his personal pronoun *I* were available too, we might see stronger influence in his life from his father than from his mother. There is a slight mixed slant between some of his letters, suggesting versatility and perhaps moodiness.

In an early signature by Vice-President Hubert Humphrey, the even, strong pressure indicates good drive and physical health; the moderate to large size, the space he took up in this world; the rhythm and right slant, his motion and direction; the continuing connections, his continuing creative thought and tenacity; and his strong forward-ending stroke, his force directed at the future.

Hubert H. Humphrey

Compare the first sample with the second sample made a few months before he died and see the breaks in rhythm and the tenaciousness with which he clung to life. The sample still exhibits his strong connections and force of character.

A *paraph* is an underscoring of the signature and indicates that the writer wants to be noticed or in the public eye. It is an assertion of *I am* and shows assertiveness, perhaps exhibitionism and/or the desire of the writer to create an effect.

The above signatures by Hubert Humphrey have a "short-cut" paraph by way of his underlining the final *Y* stroke. His paraph looks as though he is at a podium, which is an expression of his flair and need for an audience.

The following signature of Lily Pons and her paraph indicate pride, self-confidence, and her need to appear in public or be noticed. The large size depicts the room she takes up in life wherever she appears. The right slant informs her audience that she is warm and extends herself for or to them.

In addition to the paraph being an indication of assertiveness, it shows the type of personality the writer has.

Cornelia Otis Skinner's signature and paraph show her reserve by the vertical slant, but that is mitigated by the fancy, playful pedestal she creates for herself to stand on. Her heavy pressure suggests intensity, but that, too, is controlled by her strong, blunt T bar. The pastosity shows her sensuousity to sound, color, and texture.

A signature encircled proves the writer's need for protection, for secrecy, and for avoidance of intimacy. He or she may have burglar alarms, a large protective dog, or at least feel the need of such accoutrements.

An overscore has some of the same meanings that frequent arcade connections do. Imagine a writer carrying an umbrella or a shield around to protect self all of the time. This type of addition to a signature is telling the reader not to get too close, to keep your distance; the writer thinks protection.

Another "guard" type signature is one with a dot at the end of it, suggesting a mistrust of others.

Underscore by the first letter is in many cases less positive than the final backward extension. It indicates ambition but also self-admiration and selfishness.

Harry Houdini uses the *Houdini H,* from whence the name came. It is complicated though simple to make and may show his proclivity for escaping techniques. When a writer uses such an *H,* the graphologist can be certain that she gets into difficult situations of her own making but can also escape from those situations. Houdini's paraph makes a definite dramatic statement, announcing that he indeed likes being in the public eye and working from a stage, being visible to others.

8

Meaningful Letter Formations

The following pages contain some of the more widely used forms of single letters and the traits they signify arranged in alphabetical order. Shown also are model forms or styles for each letter, which are called good form samples. That doesn't necessarily mean that they are the only forms considered acceptable or positive. This listing is not meant to be an example of how everyone should make their forms. They are just examples of letters that have "good form."

Small letters carry a variety of meanings: they reveal caution, gullibility, talkativeness, generosity, and reticence. They indicate how the writer faces, and behaves in, the everyday world.

Capitals reveal a writer's taste, vulgarity, vanity, modesty, humility, rigidity, conventionality, frankness, pride, and many other traits. The larger the capital, the greater the pride of the writer. The more pride, the more the writer tends toward vanity. Smaller capitals indicate humility and modesty.

Most often if the writing is good form, a positive trait can accurately be assigned to the writing; but if poor form, the trait is more likely negative.

You will probably see many styles of letters that are not described here, but hopefully with the styles and evaluations that are presented, you will be able to assess the unknown through the known and arrive at an accurate evaluation.

Again, it is important that you not jump to a conclusion as a result of seeing one clue, but combine several different and repeated clues along with the overall picture in order to assign a meaning to the writing.

71

Some of the following distinctive styles can appear in various letters, and they mean the same wherever they appear.

a q g

Upper case made like lower case, only large in size—all letters using this activity generally mean modest or wanting to simplify.

a B C D

Narrow—shy, reserved, inhibited, symbolically squeezed; applies to all narrow upper-case letters.

a B C D

Plain, unadorned, simple—likes the simple and unadorned, straightforward in most things, and usually signifies intelligence if writing is good form.

C E J

Sharp angles—strokes that stop and change direction generally mean resentment or irresolution in some area of the writer's life. Often also means rigid, quick, clever, and realistic.

S S H

Fussy and ornate, enrolled—vulgar, bad taste, probably ostentatious, concealing.

l g y

Arc stroke back to left—indicates irresponsibility in thought or behavior, depending on letter in which it appears. Stroke goes back to past and to self.

b d h

Tall and narrow—idealistic and/or religious aspect present, as stroke reaches into the upper zone in lower-case letters.

a O O A a o

GOOD FORM SAMPLES

A's and O's are interpreted as having to do with honesty, openness, and talkativeness.

Upper Case

Garland top—often called *Lincoln A* and is considered protective and paternal.

Low cross bar—subordination.

Open at the top—open ovals usually mean talkative, honest, and open. If carried to the extreme, then probably inaccurate also.

Large knot—pride in own and/or family achievement, hanging on to a happening; also persistent, just as the pen persists in clinging to the paper.

Strokes crossed at the top—inattention to detail, inexact, just as the writer is inexact with the two strokes.

Upper case made like lower case, only large in size—all letters using this activity generally mean modest or wanting to simplify.

Narrow—shy, reserved, inhibited, symbolically squeezed.

A a O

Plain, unadorned, simple—likes the simple and unadorned, straightforward in most things, and usually signifies intelligence if writing is good form.

A

Sharp angles—strokes that stop and change direction generally mean resentment or irresolution in some area of the writer's life. Often also means rigid, quick, clever, and realistic.

A

Fussy and ornate—vulgar, bad taste, probably ostentatious.

A

Arc stroke back to left—indicates irresponsibility in thought or behavior. Stroke goes back to past and to self.

Lower Case

a o

Clean and closed—honest, reserved; if all ovals are closed, then secretive.

u o

Open at top, not tied—talkative, honest.

a o

Hook within—gross deceiver.

a o

Sharp angle—hidden greed, perhaps due to resentment.

Open bottom oval—"embezzler's oval"—lack of moral value.

Encircled and/or enrolled—selfish, dishonest, cunning, evasive.

Knotted on left—rationalizes, is not truthful with self.

Knotted on right— not totally honest with others.

Double knot—dishonest to both self and others.

Narrow knots—tells white lies.

Open—talkative but not always truthful.

Open on left—talks behind others' backs.

Covered—misrepresents self.

Dangling hook—preoccupation with sex.

$\mathcal{B}$ $\mathcal{B}$ b b

GOOD FORM SAMPLES

B's are read for expressiveness and communication.

Upper Case

 Wide bottom—gullible.

Narrow bottom—skeptical.

 Wide beginning stroke—bluffer; the wide first stroke keeps others at distance.

Reaching beginning stroke—thoughtful reaching up into the thoughtful upper zone.

 Narrow—shy, reserved, inhibited, symbolically squeezed.

Plain, unadorned, simple—likes the simple and unadorned, straightforward in most things, and usually signifies intelligence if writing is good form.

Sharp angles—strokes that stop and change direction generally mean resentment or irresolution in some area of the writer's life. Often also means rigid, quick, clever, and realistic.

Fussy and ornate—vulgar, bad taste; probably ostentatious, perhaps concealing.

Arc stroke back to left—indicates irresponsibility in thought or behavior. Stroke goes back to past and self.

Lower Case

Tall and narrow—idealistic and/or religious aspect present, as stroke reaches into the upper zone; reticent about self, unexpressive, communication about self squeezed.

Wide upper loop—imaginative, expressive. Room for thought in the upper-zone loop.

Closed upstroke—good business sense, wary, shrewd.

Short, full—humble individual who likes to talk about self; brings expressiveness into middle zone.

Without upper loop—simplifies matters regarding expression and communication; has taste and intelligence.

Circled loop—imagination and poetic taste.

GOOD FORM SAMPLES

C's are read for formation and openness. The more closed or rolled up into self the writer is, the more closed and enrolled her C appears.

Upper Case

Vertical loop—sense of responsibility toward others.

Extended upper stroke—efficient worker, directness of character, spiritual or abstract awareness.

Square—interest in building, mechanical—architects, engineers, or draftspersons often structure letters like this.

Complicated—calculating mind, just as the letter is complicated.

Encircled or enrolled—concealing.

Narrow—shy, reserved, inhibited, symbolically squeezed.

Plain, unadorned, simple—likes the simple and unadorned, straightforward in most things, and usually signifies intelligence if writing is good form.

Sharp angles—strokes that stop and change direction generally mean resentment or irresolution in some area of the writer's life. Often also means rigid, quick, clever, and realistic.

Fussy and ornate—vulgar, bad taste, probably ostentatious.

Lower Case

Beginning stroke—prop to the writer. If the stroke starts below the line, then a drive to succeed.

Plain and unadorned—idealistic, simple, gracious.

Closed—writer shields self; covering strokes are symbolic.

Pointed top—alert, curious mind as a pointed finger trying to sort out and discover the upper zone.

The c as a small, undotted i—quick-witted, probbably impatient.

Arched—simple, straightforward, constructive.

Angular bottom—resentful, insisting on own way.

GOOD FORM SAMPLES

D's are read for talkativeness, for sensitivity concerning self-conduct, and for attire and creativity.

Upper Case

Two parts—individualistic.

Broad, extended backstroke—involved in self and past, as stroke points in that direction.

Open top—frank, talkative.

Closed top—reserved, keeps own counsel.

Flying last stroke—flirtatious.

Narrow—shy, reserved, inhibited, symbolically squeezed.

Plain, unadorned, simple—likes the simple and unadorned, straightforward in most things, and usually signifies intelligence if writing is good form.

Sharp angles—strokes that stop and change direction generally mean resentment or irresolution in some area of the writer's life. Often also means rigid, quick, clever, and realistic.

Fussy and ornate—vulgar, bad taste, probably ostentatious.

Arc stroke back to left—indicates irresponsibility in thought or behavior. Stroke goes back to past and to self.

Lower Case

Tall and narrow—idealistic and/or religious aspect present, as stroke reaches into the upper zone; if stem retraced, then very dignified.

Full upper loop—thin-skinned, very sensitive. The loop in the upper zone denotes imagination regarding self. Compulsive about imagining unintentional slights.

Open bottom—unreliable and dishonest.

Open oval—talks about self.

Closed oval—secretive about individual affairs.

Low stem—humble, independent worker.

Greek—aesthetic, poetic taste, flirtatious.

Separated final stroke—"slowpoke."

Knotted—diplomatic (adjusts truth to fit situation).

Left flag—protective, musical, creative.

GOOD FORM SAMPLES

Upper Case

Stroke cutting through from left—dress is important.

Underlining stroke—self-admiration.

Starting stroke—strain in mastering affairs, life is difficult.

Concave arcs—good observer, simple approach to things, cultured, likes to read.

Upper case made like lower case, only large in size—all letters using this activity generally mean modest or wanting to simplify.

Narrow—shy, reserved, inhibited, symbolically squeezed.

Plain, unadorned, simple—likes the simple and unadorned, straightforward in most things, and usually signifies intelligence if writing is good form.

Sharp angles—strokes that stop and change direction generally mean resentment or irresolution in some area of the writer's life. Often also means rigid, quick, clever, and realistic.

Fussy and ornate—vulgar, bad taste, probably ostentatious.

Lower Case

No loop—critical, keen comprehension, quick thinker.

Narrow loop—critical, narrow-minded.

Broad loop—broadminded, willing to communicate, sometimes direct and outspoken.

Greek—likes to read; cultured, refined, aesthetic.

Final stroke going over original—garland stroke equals protectiveness, often to the extent of selfishness.

Filled in with ink—sensual.

GOOD FORM SAMPLES

F's are read for organization and planning ability.

Upper Case

Upper case made like lower case, only large in size—all letters using this activity generally mean modest or wanting to simplify.

Narrow—shy, reserved, inhibited, symbolically squeezed.

Plain, unadorned, simple—likes the simple and unadorned, straightforward in most things, and usually signifies intelligence if writing is good form.

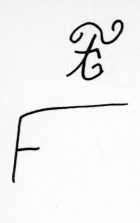

Fussy and ornate—vulgar, bad taste, probably ostentatious.

Overhanging stroke—patronizing, protective.

Lower Case

Full upper loop—articulate.

Narrow upper loop—perhaps narrow-minded.

Simple—artistic ability, intelligence, simple straightforward approach.

Angular point—resentful and uncompromising.

Angular loop—strong reaction against interference.

Cross form—concentration, fatalism.

Ink-filled—sensual.

Balanced—well-organized, managerial ability.

Big, full lower loop—food orientation, especially if pressure is also present.

Larger or longer lower loop—physical orientation, active, energetic; poor organization in some area.

Larger upper loop—mental orientation, doesn't place importance on physical aspects, poor organization in some areas.

Fluid double stroke—fluid or smooth thinker, original.

Open lower loop—austere and unconcerned about image.

Absent upper loop—forms own opinions.

G q g 8 Y y y y

GOOD FORM SAMPLES

G's are read for attitudes toward sex and basic drives; Y's, for money and materialism.

Upper Case

Greek—literary talent, has "a way with words"; cultured, aesthetic.

Upper case made like lower case, only large in size—all letters using this activity generally mean modest or wanting to simplify.

Narrow—shy, reserved, inhibited, symbolically squeezed.

Plain, unadorned, simple—likes the simple and unadorned, straightforward in most things, and usually signifies intelligence if writing is good form.

Fussy and ornate—vulgar, bad taste, probably ostentatious.

Arc stroke back to left—indicates irresponsibility in sexual and/or financial matters. Stroke goes back to past and to self.

Lower Case

Triangular loop—resentment in sexual area.

Knotted loop—twisted attitude in sex and/or money matters.

Open figure eight or long, narrow loop—restricted or twisted attitudes regarding money or sex.

Rounded, full loop—loyal, gregarious; interested in saving money.

Omission of loop bottom—in the Y, the bottom of the money bag is missing, and the writer's money just disappears due to poor saving habits.

Unfinished sharp point—resentment with repression in the sexual and material aspects of life.

Long, closed loops—strong interest in biological drives and materialistic matters.

Blunt downstroke—supervisory ability, stands on own, stubborn, independent, determined.

Long downstroke—many varied interests, restless, perhaps narrow-minded.

Small, cramped loop—selective of friends, clannish.

Large, full loop—good imagination, dramatic ability, friendly, interested in physical activity, "on display," strong libido.

Greek—literary ability, verbal fluency, fluid thinker.

Open loop—unknowledgeable or unfulfilled concerning sex and/or money.

Left arc—sexual and/or material irresponsibility.

Loop crossing below baseline—frustration in sex or money.

Left-pulled loop—abnormal attachment to mother (childhood) and/or past.

Last stroke swinging out and up—altruistic.

Falling final stroke—despondency about sex and/or money.

Upward swing to final stroke—initiative, optimism about sex and/or money.

HHh

GOOD FORM SAMPLES

H's are read for spiritual activity.

Upper Case

Houdini H—strategist, knows how to get self out of situations.

Narrow—shy, reserved, inhibited, symbolically squeezed.

Plain, unadorned, simple—likes the simple and unadorned, straightforward in most things, and usually signifies intelligence if writing is good form.

Fussy, ornate, enrolled—vulgar, bad taste, probably ostentatious.

Lower Case

High, round loop—spiritual awareness.

Left downstroke—unwilling to compromise; stroke tending back toward self.

Short upper loop—lack of thought or spiritual values.

High and narrow or retraced upper loop—opinionated, rigid, spiritual upbringing. There is no room for thought, imagination, or exploration in upper loop.

Second stroke retraced—talks about self.

GOOD FORM SAMPLES

I's are read for detail importance and punctiliousness.

The capital *I* is the ego-image, the projection of self. It indicates something of the writer's relationship with parents.

Upper Case

Narrow—shy, reserved, inhibited, symbolically squeezed.

Plain, unadorned, printed—likes the simple and unadorned, straightforward in most things, and usually signifies intelligence if writing is good form.

Straight line—mature, stands alone, aware of own value, clear and concise; may also be a disguise the writer wears in regard to feelings about parents.

Printed I *with long, full top stroke*—may mean more influence from the mother and it may be positive or negative.

Printed I *with long bottom stroke*—may mean more influence from the father, either positive or negative.

Cursive I *with upper stroke more inflated or complete than lower*—influence from mother.

Cursive I *with wider, longer, or more complete second loop*—influence from father.

Emphasis in upper zone —likes to deal with ideas or concepts, is imaginative, and sees self as beyond the ordinary.

Emphasis in the lower zone—concern with physical or material; in addition to possessions it may symbolize love of energy or power.

If emphasis is below baseline—inadequacy in relation to others.

Retraced upper loop—timid, repressed; doesn't talk about self.

Arc stroke back to left—indicates irresponsibility in thought or behavior. Stroke goes back to past and to self.

Rocking chair—acceptance of father even if he doesn't measure up to standards. He is somehow missing in writer's life. Perhaps he is a truck driver or an alcoholic, or maybe not really present at all.

Knot on second loop—forceful, talks about unpleasantness with father and has turned away from father, just as the line loops the opposite from rest of loop.

Pointed upper loop—keen mind, some resentment toward mother.

Small letter in place of capital—writer feels worthless in eyes of others.

Dollar sign—parents represent money.

Curve—takes easy way out, is not involved with life very much.

Large upper loop—talkative about self.

Crossed-out upper loop—rejects self, strict parents.

Very small in comparison with other letters—low opinion of self.

Not finished nor started well—doesn't like people.

Left-leaning—introvert, self-critic, particularly if rest of writing is right-slanted.

Right-slanted—extrovert, needs and likes people.

Far-right slant—always considers self first.

Lower Case

Dot placed far to right of stem—fast thinker, in a hurry.

High dot—good imagination, dreamer.

High, flying dot—curiosity seeker, impatience and enthusiasm.

Round, justly placed dot—detail conscious, accurate, precise, concentration.

Absence of dot—careless, absent-minded.

Circle—frustrated, attention-demanding, imaginative, artistic, individualist, dislikes routine work, likes fads, loyal to ideas and standards.

Left-faced dot—neurotic.

Right-faced dot—observant.

Flying V—sarcastic.

Tent dot—critical.

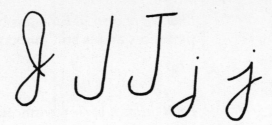

GOOD FORM SAMPLES

J's are read like the lower loops on *G*'s and *Y*'s. Lower-case *J*'s are read like lower-case *i*'s and have combined meanings.

Compare capital *J*'s to capital *I*'s; they have the same movements.

GOOD FORM SAMPLES

K's are read for attitudes regarding the opposite sex. They have to do with extroversion and introversion and feelings regarding authority.

Upper Case

Simple—mechanical, intelligent.

Second stroke higher—ambition.

Second stroke longer—bluntness, defensiveness.

Knot left of vertical bar—has had exotic past experiences and is still thinking of them.

Point through bar—resents opposite sex.

"Loving K," knot wrapped around bar—likes sex and people.

Distant second stroke—cool and distant, afraid of the opposite sex.

Second stroke just touching bar—teaser.

Lower Case

Displaced second stroke—writer does things her own way, is an independent thinker, or wants to work out problems independent of supervision. In a conversation, she may be distracted by a personal idea or thought. She may be called a rebel and seems to resent authority.

Narrow loop—opinionated.

Inflated loop—inflated, philosophical, imaginative.

Second stroke leaning—stubborn.

Rounded second stroke—yields, gives in, broadminded in argument.

Middle loop passes through bar—concerned with image and resents it.

Middle stroke doesn't reach bar—unconcerned with image.

Extended upper stroke—enterprise, reaching into upper thought zone.

GOOD FORM SAMPLES

Upper Case

Simple—cultured, artistic taste.

Missing lower loop—reserved, secretive.

Missing upper loop—positive, reserved, materialistic.

Larger base loop—self-importance, vain.

Larger upper loop—generous.

Enrolled—concealing, vulgar.

Beginning grasping arc—greedy, loves money.

Lower Case

Sharp point—penetrating mind, curious.

Broad loop—broadminded, imaginative, philosophical.

Narrow loop—opinionated, philosophical, reserved.

Straight—quick mind, sensible, intuitive.

Tall—likes to make speeches and organize.

M Mm N Nn

GOOD FORM SAMPLES

M's and N's are read for responsibility, introversion, extroversion, and communication behavior.

Upper Case

Curved beginning—good-natured, sense of humor.

Straight, horizontal beginning—dry humor.

Incurve—family pride, may hide family secret, sensitive, may dislike self.

Block—aesthetic, prefers essential only.

Vertical beginning loop ("money bag")—love of responsibility, likes to handle money.

Open bag—desires responsibility but unable to handle it.

Second stroke high—dependent on private rather than public opinion, social ambition.

Third stroke high—looks up to others, immature, envious, self-conscious.

Tapering—diplomatic, condescending.

Center downstroke short—tactless.

Squeezed—shrewd, suspicious, sizes people up.

Second stroked peaked—rude.

Sharp beginning stroke ("temper tic")—quick temper and gambler, but aboveboard gambler.

Sharp beginning stroke—"card shark," underhanded.

Lower loops present—worry about self.

Square or small horizontal beginning loop—jealous.

Lower Case

These three descriptive terms are explained in the chapter on strokes.

Garland

Arcade

Angular

Rounded—gentle, works with hands, molds, creates; logical, accumulative, analytical thinker, builds decisions on known facts.

Peaked—works with mind, bright thinker, fast comprehension, sifts facts quickly.

Final stroke pointed—quick-tempered, critical faultfinder.

Four loops—accident-prone, under mental strain.

Upper strokes looped—clairvoyance.

Lower strokes looped—worries about others.

First stroke looped—attempt to cover up worrying.

Third hump unfinished—dishonest.

Tall, peaked first stroke—pride.

Last stroke left-tending—repression, shrewdness.

Left arc—acquisitive, possessive.

O's (see A's)

GOOD FORM SAMPLES

Lower-case *P's* are read for physical activity.

Upper Case

Inflated—inflation of ego—the more inflated, the more vulnerable the writer; imaginative.

Simple—love for the beautiful, good taste, intelligence.

Original—brilliant mind, creative.

Terminal crossing over bar—reserved, discreet.

Tall—pride and vanity.

Narrow—shy, reserved, inhibited, symbolically squeezed.

Lower Case

Large loop—physical-minded, go where the action is, dancer, likes sports.

Retraced lower loop—good physical stamina and endurance, participant in sports (hiking, etc).

Short upper stem—writer unwilling to go out of the way, expects pay for favors.

High upper stem—charitable, expends energies without expecting remuneration.

p   Open bag—talks to animals or self, relaxed spending.

p   First stroke looped—argumentative, imaginative.

p   First stroke small loop—quarrelsome.

p   First stroke peaked—peaceful nature, sensitive to noise.

2 Q g g g

GOOD FORM SAMPLES

Q's are read for ovals as A's are, and the lower loops are read like Y's and J's.

GOOD FORM SAMPLES

R's are read for taste and pride, for music, and for ability with the hands.

Upper case

Narrow—shy, reserved, inhibited, symbolically squeezed.

Plain, unadorned, simple, printed—likes the simple and unadorned, straightforward in most things, and usually signifies intelligence if writing is good form.

Sharp angles—strokes that stop and change direction generally mean resentment or irresolution in some area of the writer's life. Often also means rigid, quick, clever, and realistic.

Enrolled—vulgar, bad taste, probably ostentatious.

Second stroke shorter than first—ambitious.

First stroke reaching—enterprise.

Lower Case

Large, lower-case r—dress is important to writer.

"Table top"—broadminded about religion, works with hands, skill with tools.

"Needle top"—perceptive, observant, sharp mind.

"Lazy R"—deliberate, dull, unobservant.

First stroke higher—curious, visual acuity, critical and particular.

"Parochial R"—suppressed thinking, rule follower, probably went to a private school.

Printed—able to write thoughts without difficulty.

Double peaks—finger dexterity in both hands.

Knot on first stroke—sings to self.

Knot on second stroke—sings to others.

Knots on both sides—sings to self and others.

GOOD FORM SAMPLES

Upper Case

Upper case made like lower case, only large in size— all letters using this activity generally mean modest or wanting to simplify.

Narrow—shy, reserved, inhibited, symbolically squeezed.

Plain, unadorned, simple, printed—likes the sim- ple and unadorned, straightforward in most things, and usually signifies intelligence if writing is good form.

Fussy, ornate, enrolled—vulgar, bad taste, prob- ably ostentatious.

Arc stroke back to left—indicates irresponsibility in thought or behavior. Stroke goes back to past and to self.

Treble clef—likes music, may be musical if rhythm present in writing.

Lower case

Upper peak—stubborn, investigative, curious.

Rounded top—yielding, gives in, pushover.

Closed loop—secretive.

Enrolled—shrewdness, greed.

Lower loop—tenacity.

Undulating—artistic taste.

Small capital—writer stands on ceremony, does things "according to Hoyle."

Loop on top of main body—imagination in addition to the above.

$$T \quad T \quad t \quad t$$

GOOD FORM SAMPLES

T's are read for work and ambition, among other traits.

Upper Case

Narrow—shy, reserved, inhibited, symbolically squeezed.

Plain, unadorned, simple—likes the simple and unadorned, straightforward in most things, and usually signifies intelligence if writing is good form.

Fussy, ornate, enrolled—vulgar, bad taste, probably ostentatious.

Extended bar—protective.

Lower Case
Stems

Retraced stem—repressed nature and unexpressive.

Looped stem—talkative and articulate, sensitive about work, bothered by criticism; does not do as others do just because she must conform.

Inflexible beginning stroke—resentful and stubborn.

Stem height reflects idealism

High stem—idealistic thinker, high goals.

Short stem—timid, works alone, and is often called independent worker; doesn't take chances.

Spread-out stem—slow worker, indolent.

Bar pressure shows will power

Light pressure—doesn't compete, has less will power and vitality, sensitive.

Bar begins heavy but feathers out—indecisive, gives up.

Heavy pressure—firm, tendency to always be right; good will power.

Bar height indicates goals

Bar above stem—daydreamer, shows her annoyance, unrealistic goals.

High bar—high goals, dynamic, idealistic, proud, capable, ambitious, long-range planner.

Well-balanced cross—precise, organized, self-controlled, reachable goals.

Low bar—low goals, obedience, patience, inferiority complex, humble, self-doubter.

Length of crossing indicates control

Long and sharp—sarcastic, cruel at times.

Long—enthusiastic.

Long, continuing over other letters to cross another T—mental gymnast, plans actions and efforts.

Short—underachiever, lack of control or desire for control.

Other Bars

Bowed crossing—attempts at self-control, inhibition of instinct, may want to control others.

Left-bowed crossing—attempts to control procrastination.

Shallow crossing—sense of humor, shallow thinking, easygoing, easily influenced.

"Star T"—sense of responsibility.

Star with tie—sense of responsibility but resents it; persistent, tenacious.

Whip ending—indomitable, untamable, quick temper.

Crossing back—self-pity, egotism, perhaps jealousy, possible withdrawal to past.

Cross to left—dislikes making decisions, puts off doing things, procrastinates.

Cross to right—fast thinker, impulsive, perhaps easily irritated, and on occasion, tactless.

Absent bar—absent-minded in work; careless or preoccupied and unattentive to details.

Hook on the right of bar—hanger-on, bulldog, greedy.

Changing bars—unstable in goals, control, and will power but may be versatile.

Bar with blunt downstroke—dominates and influences, determined.

Bar with tapered downstroke—bossy, domineering.

Heavy, blunt club downstroke—destructive, brutal, aggressive, determined.

Undulating downstroke—prodigious obstinacy.

Undulating bar—mimic, fun-loving, wishy-washy, frivolous, humorous.

Up-slanted bar—optimistic; if heavy, then also aggressive.

Last stroke directed up and out—easygoing, initiative, fluency, speed, unrestrictive.

Last stroke directed down—initiative not completed because of pessimistic attitude.

*Last stroke directed out but stem also crossed—*easygoing, but can suddenly become determined and willful; unpredictable.

*Hook on the left of bar—*acquisitive, needs to get work out of the way, may be possessive.

*Changing bars—*unstable in goals, control and will power, but may be versatile; perhaps a time of changing goals in writer's life.

GOOD FORM SAMPLES

*Narrow—*shy, reserved, inhibited, symbolically squeezed.

*Plain, unadorned, simple—*likes the simple and unadorned, straightforward in most things, and usually signifies intelligence if writing is good form.

*Fussy, ornate, enrolled—*vulgar, bad taste, probably ostentatious.

*Undulating beginning stroke—*sense of humor.

Lower Case

Angular—resistant.

Retraced—repressed, unexpressive.

Arcade beginning stroke—protective, fearful, appearances important.

Rounded stroke—good listener, kind, wants to be accepted.

GOOD FORM SAMPLES

Upper Case

Second stroke up and out—rebellious, resists and resents authority, enterprising.

Covering stroke—altruistic and protective.

Narrow—shy, reserved, inhibited, symbolically squeezed.

Plain, unadorned, simple—likes the simple and unadorned, straightforward in most things, and usually signifies intelligence if writing is good form.

Fussy, ornate, enrolled—vulgar, bad taste, probably ostentatious.

Lower Case

Lower-case *v* may be interpreted similarly to upper-case *v* and *u*.

GOOD FORM SAMPLES

Upper Case

Curved and sharp strokes combined in a pleasant graceful form—likes beautiful things.

Vertical loop beginning first stroke—likes responsibility.

Narrow—shy, reserved, inhibited, symbolically squeezed.

Plain, unadorned, simple—likes the simple and unadorned, straightforward in most things, and usually signifies intelligence if writing is good form.

Fussy, ornate, enrolled—vulgar, bad taste, probably ostentatious.

Wavy beginning stroke—sense of humor.

Lower Case

Tie on last stroke—poetic taste and perhaps ability.

Curved on itself—lives in past, fearful of future.

Simple—good mind, clear thinker.

Angular—analytical.

GOOD FORM SAMPLES

Upper Case

Precise cross—precision and perfection are important.

Blunt club stroke to left—stabs toward or at past, quick temper.

Curve and line—work toward future.

Separate lines—talkative, difficulty in adapting.

High right stroke—enterprise and ambition.

Narrow—shy, reserved, inhibited, symbolically squeezed.

Plain, unadorned, simple—likes the simple and unadorned, straightforward in most things, and usually signifies intelligence if writing is good form.

Fussy, ornate, enrolled—vulgar, bad taste, probably ostentatious.

Lower Case

Read the same as for upper case.

Y's are read as G's.

GOOD FORM SAMPLES

Upper Case

Underlining stroke—self-admiration.

Narrow—shy, reserved, inhibited, symbolically squeezed.

Plain, unadorned, simple—likes the simple and unadorned, straightforward in most things, and usually signifies intelligence if writing is good form.

Fussy, ornate, enrolled—vulgar, bad taste, probably ostentatious.

Curved—easygoing.

Downstroke unfinished—doesn't finish things; perhaps there is depression or fatigue.

Lower Case

Read as for upper case.

9

Doodles

For years I have wondered about the doodles on the walls of telephone booths, in phone books, on table cloths, place mats, billboards, posters, books, and every kind of paper. During a trip to the Great Wall in China I even saw a very old doodle on one of the blocks that make up the wall. Not being able to read it, I asked a guide what it said. He informed me that it didn't really say anything, that forms had just been chiseled into the rock with the meanings known only to the chiseler. If it really was a doodle, perhaps even the chiseler didn't really know why she had left the forms she had. The meanings of those doodles were always a curiosity to me until graphology appeared in my life. They now seem less a mystery but continue to arouse my curiosity about the varied expressions of human complexities.

Doodles are a means for the subject to release tension, anxiety and/or frustration, or they might symbolize whatever the doodler is absorbed in at the moment. They come directly from a level of consciousness that is different from normal, and the doodler most likely has no idea why her doodles develop the way they do. Doodling is an abstract thought condensed into an image or symbol; it is a language of imagery and symbology. Since each of our views regarding symbols and images comes from our past experience and our past experiences all vary, it is expected that the symbology will vary. Indeed it does vary, but only somewhat. I will review some of the common symbols that serve as guides to help you learn to interpret your own doodles.

Most people doodle at some time or another. Since doodling is an acceptable, covert way to express frustration and release tension, it is a common activity. Some people are frequent doodlers and others are only occasionally, depending on their past and present. A newly engaged woman might doodle her fiance's name or images of wedding rings. It is a pleasant doodle because it is a pleasant time in her life, and it is a symbol of her absorption. If it is shaded or darkened it may be an expression of unspoken anxiety.

Doodles project the doodler's looks, thoughts, feelings, and behavior. They are all self-portraits. The more complicated the doodle, the more complicated the doodler, her images of herself, and the situation in which she sees herself existing.

The practice of duplicating certain strokes or whole doodles and forcing awareness of your own feelings is as valuable in doodle analysis as it is in handwriting analysis. Feel emotionally with your fingertips as you repeat the motions. Doodle a staircase. Notice the firmness with which you draw. Is there a feeling of decisiveness? If so, you are probably using firm strokes. Are the steps exact? That might signal that you feel exact. Did you start from the bottom, ascending and climbing with high aspirations, or did you start at the top, moving down into materialism or basic drives, giving attention to a different kind of survival? Consider and study how this effort affects you as you construct.

LEFT MIDDLE RIGHT

UPPER ZONE		
MIDDLE ZONE		
LOWER ZONE		

Using the geographical principles of space and placement of ink within that space, imagine the material upon which the doodle is placed as a rectangle with an upper, middle, and lower zone. Imagine also left, middle, and right areas so that you have roughly nine areas. If the doodle is placed in the horizontal upper zone, it corresponds to the emphasis on upper-zone writing. If placed in the middle, then emphasis is on the middle zone, and if in the lower third of the material, the correspondence is to the lower zone.

If we remember that vertical left corresponds to introversion, self, past, and mother, that the middle corresponds to the present, and that the right corresponds to extroversion, others, future, and father, it is possible to begin to assign meanings to the doodle by its placement. As in graphology, the analyst must assess all of the clues, applying more meaning to the strongest or most frequent but never ignoring the weaker.

If a choice of pen or pencil is available, the doodler's choice also offers clues to her personality. The choice of a pencil might point to the doodler giving herself a chance to change her mind and erase the doodle if she so desires. Remembering that all doodles are projections of self, a pencil drawing might show the doodler being dissatisfied with self, wanting to make sure that she can change what she is now. Indecisiveness would probably sum up such a tendency. An inked collection of symbols show where the doodler is firmly entrenched.

Shaded-in areas signal aggression, resentment, or particular tension, and the more pressure shown, the more the repressed anger. Heavy pressure points to serious thought, intensity, and perhaps determination, seriousness, or sadness.

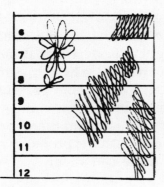

Light, single strokes are more forgiving, accepting, sensitive, friendly and averse to friction; they show a desire for peace.

Many of the symbols in our culture have common beginnings. For example, the sun. To all cultures, that which gives light, the sun, is seen as a positive image. This is true in doodles. A doodler who doodles the sun is doodling a positive image. The other factor that makes it positive is the circular motion creating it. Circular motions are much easier to make than angular and generally indicate adaptability and sensitivity.

Right-slanted doodles, or blueprints of the unconscious, indicate progressiveness, extroversion, and new ideas.

Left slants might show caution, hesitancy, or secretive moods. The shape of this doodle shows a practical, intelligent, logical mind.

This doodle looks to the left, which is past and self. Since doodles also are drawings of the doodler, this might indicate a very attractive woman involved in herself, perhaps selfish and with some present involvement in the past. Since the pressure is slight and there is minimal shading, this is probably not a sign of repressed anger.

A variety of slants, just as in handwriting, points to versatility and perhaps inconsistency in behavior. This doodle was placed exactly in the middle of the top of the paper.

Size shows ego, ambition, and measure of self-esteem. Animals denote a love of the outdoors and animals, or those smaller and weaker.

Curved strokes are easier to make and cause less friction, and they have the same meanings that curved strokes or garlands do in handwriting. The behavior revealed is more passive and flexible than that shown by hard, rigid strokes.

Angular strokes probably show construction of something, criticism, aggressiveness, or self-reliance. The pressure in the more complicated doodle may be a clue to a more intense, determined individual.

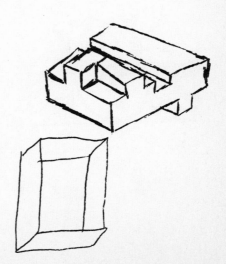

Toothpick-people drawings are probably symbols of the doodler. They might indicate a desire for attention and perhaps a swollen ego. If the figure has a bent back, a short leg, or is minus an arm, look for a like defect in the doodler or a sense of not being complete.

Ugly faces might announce a paranoia or fear, a dislike of people or of self. These two doodles were done without lifting the pen from the paper, which would be a sign of strong persistence.

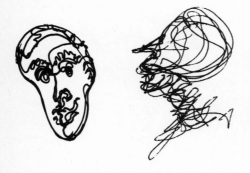

The addition of moustaches, glasses, or similar contributions to an already finished product is a sign of a bossy "driver's seat" doodler, one who desires authority and doesn't have much.

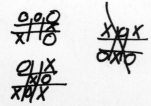

Tic-tac-toe symbols show a liking for competition, expanded thinking, and probably a real planner.

A doodler who repeatedly draws lovely eyes is a lover of beauty and is impressed by such.

Doodling body parts may indicate an interest in that body part—perhaps an illness or an unusually prominent feature. A crossed-out figure could tell that the doodler is very fussy or feels like crossing out self.

This design of flowers, fruit, a wine glass, and an insect nest with very light pressure announces a gentle, caring doodler who is feeling threatened. The threat may be from a boring speaker at a meeting being attended, or it could be something more serious. The light shading is describing some tension or stress.

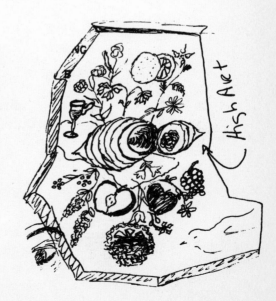

Tiny feet probably are many doodlers' subconscious way of expressing insecurity. If there is a floor beneath the feet, it might be interpreted as an attempt to build up or stabilize the feeling of insecurity.

Birds show consideration of the doodler for others, love of freedom and the outdoors, and probably a gentle and affectionate nature.

Check marks most likely pinpoint the doodler as a skeptic—not only of others' ideas but of her own. This person may need encouragement to succeed.

Bracket drawers study facts and are problem solvers.

Decreasing ovals are signs of repression and a fear of taking risks. Such a person is probably not comfortable with initiating projects.

Spider webs often express a desire to move around more, to get out of a trap. The spider is facing inward toward the center of the web, although not in the middle. The doodler may feel she is being drawn deeper and deeper into the web or an area that prevents the expansion she would like.

Whimsical with dark, sad eyes—a portrait of the doodler.

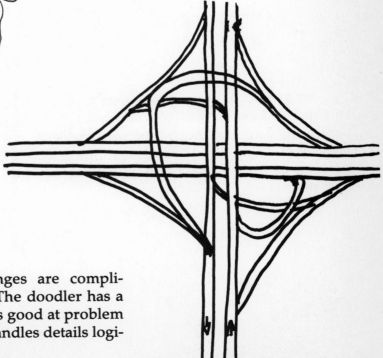

Freeway interchanges are complicated and engrossing. The doodler has a sharp, agile mind and is good at problem solving. He probably handles details logically and reasonably.

Clowns across the top of the meeting agenda could show the bored doodler trying to inject a little humor into her life at the moment. The clowns' varying position on and below the lines but with pleasant expressions on their faces may have no significance unless it would be poor planning or not knowing how big they were going to be when they were finished.

An artistic creation, this object took patience and skill at design to form. The dark, shaded areas show irritation or anger but the rounding is gentle and easy. Since a felt-tip pen was used, it is hard to evaluate pressure.

Shoes, legs, and feet shown amid wheeled vehicles is either the artist planning a trip or a move or wanting to plan such. The shading might be irritation at the slow progress of the meeting being attended or irritation regarding plans for the trip.

Logical reasoning is shown by these types of forms. The doodler's fertile mind comes up with many ingenious ideas, but he is not impulsive and may not even follow through.

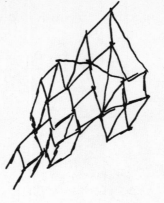

This doodler thinks in a constructive manner and is probably inclined to be stubborn. He is able to give attention to detail and prefers to think for himself.

Patience is one of the obvious signs this doodle represents. She can take on a task and work to its finish in a smooth, patient, careful fashion.

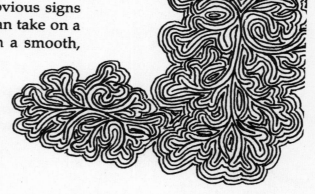

Have fun and enjoy the meanings suggested above. Be aware that there are many factors that go into these expressions and that they vary just as personalities vary because of the programming of the individual by the past.

10

Utilization

A few of the uses of graphology will be mentioned in a very limited way in the material that follows. In addition to these uses there are a number of others, including compatibility studies, criminology, forensic graphology, and jury screening. I expect there are probably several others, and I am aware that a graphologist is limited only by lack of initiative.

Graphotherapy

The word *graphotherapy* was first used in France in the early 1930s. It comes from the Greek word *graph*, meaning "written," and *therapy*, meaning "treatment" or "healing." Dr. Edgar Berillon, a psychologist, first promoted the theory that by changing writing, behavior would also change. Professor Charles Henry and Dr. Pierre Janet thoroughly tested this theory at the Sorbonne, in Paris, and their results seemed to prove that the theory was indeed a fact.

The most noted graphotherapists in the United States were the late Paul de Sainte Colombe and his wife Kathi Lanier de Sainte Colombe. Their published book, *Grapho-Therapeutics*, is a guidebook describing their work and research.

To quote the Colombes, "You can correct your worst faults and strengthen your character by changing your handwriting." It is a widely held belief that each time a writer makes a stroke that supports a negative habit or attitude she is also reinforcing this habit or belief.

One of the problems in the field of graphotherapy is that often there are people who claim to be graphotherapists who have not yet reached a competence in their practice. Although there probably are many practicing graphotherapists who are competent, there are, unfortunately, also many incompetents. Should a reader desire to experiment with self, that is her privilege; but to claim competence and prescribe for others is a serious error in judgment unless the reader has a strong background in counseling as well as in graphology and perhaps psychology.

The information that follows is strictly for experimentation with self, and under no circumstances should it be used in prescribing changes in another's writing for the purposes of changing behavior and/or attitude.

The practice of graphotherapy is a conscious alteration of various factors in the handwriting designed to retrain the writer in different writing characteristics, which will at the same time retrain the writer's habits and/or attitudes.

Some of the following suggestions are adapted from *Grapho-Therapeutics.*

1. Find a comfortable place to sit, such as a table or desk, with enough room for your writing arm to rest on the surface near your paper.

2. Use your favorite, most comfortable pen.

3. Schedule practice sessions at least twice a day that will be free from other commitments.

4. Write a sentence that is a positive statement, is fairly short, uses the personal pronoun *I,* and supports the change that you are going to make. In these sentences concentrate on what you want to gain or become rather than on what habit or behavior you want to be rid of. Examples of positive sentences are

> a. I experience and maintain inner peace of mind.
> b. My mind and body heal themselves continuously.
> c. I am master of my fate, and life is what I make it.
> d. I am positive and I associate and surround myself with positive, uplifting individuals.
> e. The only thing I have to fear is fear itself.
> f. I have the will power to accomplish the things I want to do.

5. Select only one trait at a time that you wish to change. As you progress you can choose others, but don't try and change too much at the beginning.

6. On each practice sheet make sure that you number or date your writing so that you can monitor your progress and make changes if necessary.

7. Exaggerate the change the first few times you write the sentence but gradually let it become a natural part of your writing.

8. It is advisable that you write the sentence during each practice session from eight to ten times.

9. Watch your practice sheets carefully, noticing how well you are effecting the changes desired.

Do not become discouraged. The trait you are trying to change has probably been with you for a long time and may not leave readily.

Psychological Counseling

Psychological counseling is another utilization of graphology. Psychologists, social workers holding an MSW, and experienced, qualified counselors from one of the many counseling fields will find the addition of graphological skills an important tool. Graphology is a valid, useful tool but it is only one more instrument to use for better understanding a client. It is not a means unto itself! That means that just because an individual has mastered many rudiments of graphology does not make her an expert in "helping folks." Most graphologists who counsel clients have been educated and supervised in some other field of counseling or have been associated with counseling in some way. Psychologists may rely on graphologists to do a profile of a client's personality to help identify hidden problem areas.

To those readers who read this as a discouragement to practicing their skills, please be aware that it is meant as an encouragement to broaden your skills through approved educational paths or, as mentioned above, to gain more information by assisting those who are qualified in psychological counseling.

Fun

Graphology is fun, interesting, and informative, and after practicing the skill on yourself you will no doubt be requested to practice your skills on your friends. You may find yourself the center of many social groups.

Some helpful hints follow for use in social situations in which you find yourself sharing your graphological skills.

1. Never accept a sample from someone who has been talked into providing one. The writer, in addition to resenting those who insisted on the analysis, will probably resent you, too, and it is an invasion of privacy.

2. Never do someone's sample who is not present. That is also an invasion of privacy, and if not illegal, it probably should be.

3. Avoid getting too serious, as it doesn't fit well at parties with others present.

If you have been hired as a professional to entertain at a gathering by using your graphological skills, the above suggestions remain true, plus the following:

4. Schedule a limited time for each partygoer and stick to it. It is wise to

have a clock or watch where you can see it to keep track of the time.

5. Again, to stress #3 above: There will be many guests who expect you not only to reveal their habits and characteristics to them but also to tell them how to manage their lives and problems. Avoid any advice. Just tell them what their writing indicates to you.

6. Be prepared with single, uncomplicated writing characteristics which, although they need other factors to substantiate them, are often accurate and enjoyed by the writer being analyzed. Some of the following examples may be helpful.

a. sings or hums out loud to others

b. sings or hums out loud to self

c. likes to argue

d. strong will power

e. protective of self and loved ones

f. good listener

g. ambitious

h. independent

i. proud

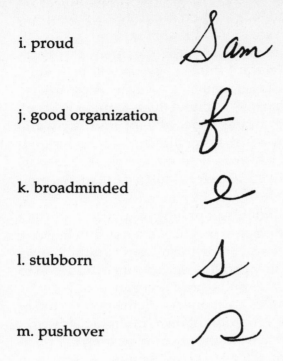

j. good organization

k. broadminded

l. stubborn

m. pushover

When doing "quickies," which of course lack the validity that a more lengthy analysis would have, it is important to remember that the absence of a clue such as those mentioned above does not mean that the writer does not have such a trait. The trait may show up elsewhere in the writing. The absence has no meaning whatsoever. For instance, a writer may not make the small balloon on the right of a small *r* and yet still sing out loud to others. Only its presence is of value when giving an evaluation.

As noted before, graphology can be fun; but to make sure that you do not abuse your knowledge, be aware that it can be a serious invasion of a writer's privacy if not used with respect and consideration.

Personnel Selection

For many years knowledgeable managers have been using graphology as one of their tools to improve hiring practices and placement of employees. Many people who have had experience sifting through written applications and interviewing prospective employees come, perhaps unknowingly, to an informal understanding of graphology. After reading resumes and interviewing applicants, a connection between certain types of personalities and how they write is often assimilated and used to help in evaluations. This skill, although useful, cannot compare to a studied, thorough, professional written evaluation furnished by a professional graphologist.

In the September 3, 1985 *Wall Street Journal*, the chairman of a Paris, France bank is quoted as saying, "Even if I think a person will be good, I won't take him if our graphologist advises against it." A Paris executive recruiter informed the same *Journal* reporter, "At least 80 percent of France's biggest companies use graphology in hiring, especially for executives and professionals." Another statement by a managing director affirms his dedication to the use of this versatile skill: "A study of new employees chosen by this method, after their first year, showed 80 percent turned out just as their handwriting analysis predicted."

It needs to be understood that although graphology is a very important tool, it should not and cannot take the place of practices such as the checking of prospective employees' references and credentials. Many graphologists are also trained to use other personality profile instruments in addition to graphology to achieve an even more complete and accurate profile.

Hopefully, the handwriting samples are gained with the permission of the prospective employee or candidate for promotion. Graphologists working in personnel selection request data from the client regarding the position for which the writer is being considered, including a job description and any other pertinent facts available.

For example, some basic qualities important for a supervisory position and some writing traits supporting these qualities (in addition to good form) are

1. decisiveness—firm, sudden endings; evidence of at least some angle connections and moderate to heavy pressure.

2. leadership—little space between words; slightly concave lines; firm pressure and sizeable script.

3. judiciousness—vertical letter slant; fair symmetry and good rhythm.

4. initiative—right letter slant; some letters unconnected and slightly convex lines.

5. adaptability—flexible garland connections; good rhythm and moderate to light pressure.

For the inexperienced graphologist there will probably be conflict in integrating all of the writing traits suggested above. When traits are in conflict, they must be weighed one against the other to arrive at an accurate result. For example, a trait that appears frequently in a writing will certainly be a stronger personality trait in the writer than one that appears only occasionally. And there are certainly additional personality traits important for a supervisor. Instant handwriting analysis is very often not possible in personnel selection. The subject is deep and complex and the sparse information offered above barely touches it.

For study in this expanding field of employment analysis, I recommend the book *Advanced Graphology* by Betty Link.

Graphopathology

Another utilization of graphology is in the field known as graphopathology, or the study of handwriting as an aid in the diagnosis of diseases.

Much has been written regarding the psychological state of the mind as reflected in handwriting, but much less has been written regarding the *physiological* state as reflected in handwriting.

One of the researchers of illness as reflected in handwriting is Alfred Kanfer, a noted graphologist who studied the handwriting of cancer patients for many years. To quote Kanfer, "The pen-stroke of the normal, healthy person is reasonably smooth and continuous, and this can easily be established under a microscope.

"If, however, cancer or a precancerous situation exists in the person, his pen-strokes are not smooth. They look like the zigzag-edged body of a caterpillar.

"The zigzags are very delicate in the beginning but they gradually become rougher as the condition progresses. The pressure on the pen and the flow of the ink seems to be broken by minute muscle twitches. This suggests the malfunctioning of the nerve impulses that run from the brain to the muscles. However, these twitches are so tiny that they can neither be felt by the person nor recognized by the naked eye. They must not be confused with a simple shaking hand, due usually to a nervous condition or old age."

The Metropolitan Insurance Company requested Kanfer to do a large-scale study of 935 handwriting samples, of which 88 had cancer. He was 84 percent correct in diagnosing those with cancer.

Unfortunately, his revolutionary theories are still not easily accepted in this country and are vehemently opposed by many. Mr. Kanfer is now deceased, and to my knowledge there are no serious, funded studies being carried out using his theories.

Each graphologist interested in graphopathology perhaps has her own theories or ways of recognizing illness through handwriting. Leslie King states in her manual, *Physical Health and Illness in Handwriting* (no longer available), that the line of writing reflects both the flow of blood and breathing. She continues to inform that dots on the ductus, or line, indicate collections of blood at that location in the body. I have not personally researched this theory at any time.

If the sample shows inconsistent pressure, wandering baselines, uneven spacing, and general degeneration throughout, then after careful study one might guess at a systemic disease such as leukemia, high blood pressure, anemia, malnutrition, or diabetes.

I am not aware that alcoholism can be diagnosed using graphology, but some indications that might appear are descending lines, shakiness due to a trembling hand, and an inconsistency and/or weakness in the T bars.

In my experience, it is difficult to tell how long a disturbance has affected the writer. The disturbance may no longer cause any pain or visible deformity, but the body retains the memory and reflects that memory.

In studying the handwriting for clues to the physical body, the zones are quite specific in indicating location. It was mentioned earlier that handwriting is very symbolic. Nowhere is that more important than in graphopathology. Imagine, for a moment, that a letter in the sample is the body of the writer: The lower zone in the writing corresponds to the legs and feet, the middle zone to trunk, and the upper zone to upper trunk and head.

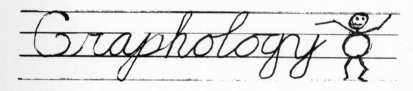

head and upper trunk

trunk

legs and feet

An unusual twist to the end of a T bar may indicate a present or past arm or shoulder injury. This writer had broken a bone in his upper arm several years ago.

A leg recently broken and healed may look no different than one broken 40 years ago in childhood. This and any leg or foot injury would probably be reflected in indented, sharp, or missing strokes in the lower loops of G's or Y's. This writer had a piece of shrapnel removed from his left lower leg three years previously. He did not limp.

A sharpness or flatness in the upper zone might indicate a past or present head injury or maybe even a headache, while a projection could be the clue to a tumor. A break or missing part of a stroke might also suggest the loss of an eye.

A capital *G* with accentuation on the first loop shows the right eye to be dominant. Accentuation on the second loop indicates the left eye is dominant. If there is a congenital problem with one eye, the emphasis reverses. A deficient left eye with a stronger right eye will have the emphasis on the right.

Capital *E*'s represent the ears. Again, this is a theory that I have not personally researched, but other graphologists state that the top stroke of a "cultured" *E* signifies the right ear, and if closed or deformed it indicates that the right ear is deficient, painful, or diseased. The second, or bottom, stroke is said to indicate difficulty in the left ear. The number 3 also has the same strokes as the cultured *E*. I would expect that the traits symbolized by the number 3 would also translate the same as the cultured *E*.

Cardiac disorders may cause sudden slight jerks in the person as the heart fails to beat steadily. The writing of heart attack victims often has consistent breaks in the upper zone. I have personally observed many such samples, and the break or ragged line may also appear as a concave stroke. It seems to appear in different places depending on the location of the vessel involved. This sample was written several months before the writer had a heart attack.

When you consider the appearance of diseased blood vessels in the heart of a victim, you can see the symbology. The vessel causing the heart failure has usually gradually become sclerosed or occluded, as the diagram shows. When the plaque becomes large enough it shuts off the flow of blood to a specific area that nourishes that part of the heart. The victim's handwriting often graphically displays this action.

Both Max Pulver in *The Symbology of Handwriting* and Paul de Sainte Colombe in *Grapho-Therapeutics* describe a cross under the base of the signature as being a clue to suicidal tendencies.

If looking for these graphic displays, it is wise to see many of them before making an evaluation. If only one display of a disturbance is evident, it may be that the writer was writing on a crumb or an uneven surface, which has nothing to do with a physical situation.

The few statements above are in no part meant to guide a student into the practice of graphopathology, but only to inform her of another of the many directions the study of graphology can take.

11

Special Uses

Questioned Document

Questioned document specialists can be much in demand. Although having a graphological background may be helpful to an aspiring document examiner, it isn't necessary. But a graphologist without special training and/or experience in examining documents is a detriment to the science of graphology if offering services without proper background.

To quote Janice Klein, who is treasurer of the National Bureau of Document Examiners: "Whereas graphology interprets character from handwriting, questioned document examination determines the authorship of disputed handwritings and signatures on all kinds of documents—wills, leases, contracts, etc. A questioned document examiner usually has his or her own private practice, but will work for a wide variety of clients, such as lawyers, individuals, banks, the government, etc.

"In order to become court qualified, which is the distinction we make between Professional and Associate levels, the examiner must have been accepted by a judge in court."

There are a number of schools listed in the Appendix that offer studies in the field, but there is apparently some conflict between the graphologically prepared questioned document examiners and those who are certified through the American Society of Questioned Document Examiners. Among requirements for this certification are a college degree and from three to four years apprenticeship with an experienced examiner. The type of degree is unspecified. (Just as in graphology, there are no college degrees offered in questioned document examination.) There also are training courses available through the Secret Service and the Federal Bureau of Investigation. There are no graphology requirements for this certification.

Although as far as I know there isn't a permanent address for the American Society of Questioned Document Examiners, there is one for the American Academy of Forensic Sciences, whose members also are not required to have any graphology background or experience. The address for the American Academy of Forensic Sciences and the National Bureau of Document Examiners is listed in the Appendix.

Child Development

This utilization is also a specialized field, but the general principles of graphology do hold true here. A graphologist wishing to become involved in this area needs some in-depth background in child, adolescent, and developmental psychology. A skilled graphologist can often diagnose disabling diseases such as schizophrenia and initiate treatment and early support programs. Teachers often study and practice graphology to supplement their other skills after having noticed a correlation between variations of a student's handwriting and personality patterns.

Many children are first taught printing and then cursive writing. Either stage of learning will contain elements for the experienced graphologist to study and research.

Vocational Appraisal and Career Counseling

Employment counselors will find knowledge of graphology helpful in dealing with their clients. A client whose large, disorganized writing with long, full, lower loops may wonder why working alone in a sedentary position is not a fulfilling job. Perhaps just because such a position satisfied the client's father is no reason for it to satisfy this individual, and a trained graphologist could realize this immediately upon seeing the writing and counsel the client accordingly.

A skilled graphologist can discern if clients can tolerate tedious, monotonous work or if they will function better in a less restricted position. She can also easily weed out followers applying for leadership positions.

Writing that might suggest dishonesty would discourage a counselor from making a recommendation of the writer for a cashier or teller job.

A graphologist may be called upon to do individual vocational appraisals for clients dissatisfied with their own haphazard choices. An employment agency might contract with a graphologist to serve the graphological needs of a whole office or might call one in for specific cases.

Intelligence Determination

An experienced graphologist can usually ascertain the level of a writer's intelligence. Some of the factors that can be investigated and scored are organization, simplification, originality, expressiveness, and rhythm.

A published paper describing a scoring method using those factors is called *I.Q. from Handwriting* by Charlie Cole. The resulting numerical score compares favorably to I. Q. scores obtained through other well-known methods of testing.

Appendix

Schools

Handwriting Consultants International (HCI)
11481 Caminito Garcia
San Diego, CA 92131
Telephone (619) 586-1511

The Institute of Graphological Science (tIGS)
3685 Ingleside
Dallas, TX 75229
Telephone (214) 351-3668

Manhattan Handwriting Consultant
Felix Klein
250 West 57th Street, Suite 2032
New York, NY 10107
Telephone (212) 265-1148

The above-listed schools offer various courses, many by correspondence, including basic to advanced handwriting analysis, vocational guidance, personnel selection, document examination, graphotherapy, graphopathology, chemical abuse, and personal worth. Listings and costs may be received by telephoning or writing them at the addresses listed above.

According to Marjorie Westergaard in *Directory of Handwriting Analysts*, there are a number of accredited schools offering credit courses in graphology. She lists schools in New Jersey, Massachusetts, New York, and California.

The Institute of Graphological Science is licensed by the Texas State Education Agency and has been since 1983. As far as I have been able to discover, it is the only graphological school that is state licensed.

Professional Organizations

American Association of Handwriting Analysts (AAHA)
820 West Maple Street
Hinsdale, IL 60521
Telephone (312) 325-2266

American Handwriting Analysis Foundation (AHAF)
P.O. Box 6201
San Jose, CA 95150

Council of Graphological Societies (COGS)
904 South Belgrade Drive
Silver Spring, MD 20902
Telephone (301) 649-3637

Handwriting Analysts International (HAI)
1504 West 29th Street
Davenport, IA 52804

Handwriting Consultants International (HCI)
11481 Caminito Garcia
San Diego, CA 92131
Phone (619) 586-1511

The International Graphological Society (tIGS)
3685 Ingleside
Dallas, TX 75229
Telephone (214) 351-3668

National Society for Graphology
National Bureau of Document Examiners (NBDE)
250 West 57th Street, Suite 2032
New York, NY 10107
Telephone (212) 265-1148

American Academy of Forensic Sciences
225 S. Academy Blvd.
Colorado Springs, CO 80910

Bibliography

Colombe, Paul de Sainte. *Grapho-Therapeutics*. Hollywood, CA: Laurida Books Publishing Co., 1969.

Green, Jane Nugent. *You and Your Private "I."* 3rd ed. St. Paul, MN: Llewellyn Publications, 1988.

Green, Jane Nugent. *The I's Have It: A Collection of Papers on the Personal Pronoun I.* For information regarding either of the two above publications, contact Jane Nugent Green, 1760 Summit Avenue, St. Paul, Minnesota 55105.

Kanfer, Alfred. *A Guide to Handwriting Analysis*. New York: Dell, 1962.

Karohs, Dr. Erika. *Encyclopedia for Handwriting Analysts*. For information, write author at P.O. Box 1476, Pebble Beach, CA 93953.

King, Leslie W. *Physical Health and Illness in Handwriting* (no longer available).

Klages, Ludwig. *Handwriting and Character*. Leipzig, 1940.

Link, Betty. *Advanced Graphology*. 1988. For brochure describing book and cost, contact Betty Link, P.O. Box 48912, Chicago, IL 60648-0912.

Mendel, Alfred O. *Personality in Handwriting*. New York: Stephen Daye, 1947.

Olyanova, Nadya. *Psychology of Handwriting*. Hollywood, CA: Wilshire Book Co., 1960.

Pulver, Max. *Symbology of Handwriting*. Zurich, 1940.

Roman, Klara G. *Handwriting, A Key to Personality.* New York: Noonday Press, 1962.

Rosen, Billie. *Science of Handwriting Analysis.* New York: Bonanza Books, 1965.

Westergaard, Marjorie. *Directory of Handwriting Analysts.* 7th ed., 1988. This directory has a listing of schools offering credits in graphology, proprietary schools, professional graphological organizations, libraries, individual listings of graphologists, and graphology journals and newsletters. It can be ordered at a cost of $12.95 from the author: 31246 Wagner, Warren, Michigan 48093.

Cole, Charlie. *I.Q. from Handwriting.* Available from author: 1166 El Solyo Avenue, Campbell, CA 95008.

Index

STAY IN TOUCH...
Llewellyn publishes hundreds of books on your favorite subjects

On the following pages you will find listed some books now available on related subjects. Your local bookstore stocks most of these and will stock new Llewellyn titles as they become available. We urge your patronage.

ORDER BY PHONE
Call toll-free within the U.S. and Canada, **1–800–THE MOON**.

In Minnesota call **(612) 291–1970**.

We accept Visa, MasterCard, and American Express.

ORDER BY MAIL
Send the full price of your order (MN residents add 7% sales tax) in U.S. funds to :

Llewellyn Worldwide,
P.O Box 64383, Dept. L251-9
St. Paul, MN 55164–0383, U.S.A.

POSTAGE AND HANDLING
(for the U.S., Mexico, and Canada)
- $4.00 for orders $15.00 and under
- $5.00 for orders over $15.00
- No charge for orders over $100.00

We ship UPS in the continental United States. We ship standard mail to P.O. boxes. Orders shipped to Alaska, Hawaii, the Virgin Islands and Puerto Rico are sent first-class mail.

Orders shipped to Canada or Mexico are sent surface mail. Surface mail: Add $1.00 per item.

International orders: Airmail—add freight equal to price of each book to the total price of order, plus $5.00 for each non-book item (audiotapes, etc.).

Allow 4–6 weeks delivery on all orders. Postage and handling rates subject to change.

GROUP DISCOUNTS
We offer a 20% quantity discount to group leaders or agents. You must order a minimum of 5 copies of the same book to get our special quantity price.

Free Catalog
Get a free copy of our color catalog, *New Worlds of Mind and Spirit*. Subscribe for just $10.00 in the United States and Canada ($30.00 airmail). Many bookstores carry *New Worlds*—ask for it!

READING BETWEEN THE LINES
The Basics of Handwriting Analysis
P. Scott Hollander

Anyone who reads and follows the procedures in *Reading Between the Lines* will come away with the ability to take any sample of handwriting and do a complete analysis of character and personality. He or she may even go forward to use the skill as a professional tool, or as the basis for a profession.

Handwriting analysis can help you gain insight into your own strengths and weaknesses and can provide a means to make wiser decisions in your personal and professional life. You will have a quick, sure means of discovering what someone else is really like, and you can use graphotherapy to effect character and personality changes.

Reading Between the Lines also contains an excellent section on the writing of children, and an Index of Traits which summarizes and reiterates points made in the book for quick reference.

0-87542-309-4, 272 pp., 7 x 10, illus., softcover **$14.95**

INSTANT PALM READER
A Road Map to Life
Linda Domin

The road of your life is mapped out on the palm of your hand. When you know how to interpret the information, it is like seeing an aerial view of all the scenes of your life that you will travel. You will get candid, uplifting revelations about yourself: personality, childhood, career, finances, family, love life, talents and destiny. Author Linda Domin has upgraded and modernized the fine art of palmistry. By decoding all the palm-lines systems of the major schools of palmistry and integrating them with her own findings, she has made it possible for anyone to assemble a palm reading that can be trusted for its accuracy.

This book was specifically designed to answer those personal questions unanswerable by conventional methods. Using this exciting method of self-discovery, you can now uncover your hidden feelings and unconscious needs as they are etched upon the palm of your hand.

0-87542-162-8, 256 pp., 7 x 10, illus., softcover **$14.95**

PALMISTRY
The Whole View
Judith Hipskind

Here is a unique approach to palmistry! Judy Hipskind not only explains how to analyze hands, but also explains why hand analysis works. The approach is based on a practical rationale and is easy to understand. Over 130 illustrations accompany the informal, positive view of hand analysis.

This new approach to palmistry avoids categorical predictions and presents the meaning of the palm as a synthesis of many factors: the shape, gestures, flexibility, mounts and lives of each hand—as well as a combination of the effects of both heredity and the environment. No part of the hand is treated as a separate unit; the hand reflects the entire personality. An analysis based on the method presented in this book is a rewarding experience for the client—a truly whole view!

0-87542-306-X, 248 pp., 5¼ x 8, illus., softcover $12.95

REVEALING HANDS
How to Read Palms
Richard Webster

Palmistry has been an accurate tool for self-knowledge and prediction for thousand of years. The ability to read palms can lead you to a better understanding of yourself, as well as the complex motivations of other people. Guide and advise others in a sensitive and caring manner, determine compatibility between couples, and help people decide what type of career suits them best.

Revealing Hands makes it is easier than ever to learn the science of palmistry. As soon as you complete the first chapter, you can begin reading palms with confidence and expertise. Professional palmist and teacher Richard Webster leads you step-by-step through the subject with clear explanations and life-size hand drawings that highlight the points being covered. He provides sample scripts that can serve as a foundation for your readings for others, and he answers all of the questions he has been asked by his students over the years. Whether you are interested in taking up palmistry professionally or just for fun, you will find the information in this book exceptionally entertaining and easy to use.

0-87542-870-3, 304 pp., 7 x 10, 117 illus., softcover $14.95